The House of Skulls

A Partial List of Publications by M & J Grand Orbit

1. *Four Decades in the Study of Languages & Linguistics in Nigeria*
2. *In the Linguistic Paradise*
3. *Languages & Culture in Nigeria*
4. *Trends in the Study of Language & Linguistics in Nigeria*
5. *Convergence: English and Nigeria Languages*
6. *Language, Literature and Culture in Nigeria*
7. *Language Policy, Planning & Management in Nigeria*
8. *Language, Literature & Communication in Nigeria*
9. *Language, Literature & Culture in a Multilingual Society*
10. *Issues in Contemporary African Linguistics*
11. *Globalization & the Study of Languages in Africa*
12. *Numeral Systems of Nigerian Languages*
13. *The Syntax of Igbo Causatives: A Minimalist Account*
14. *English Studies and National Development*
15. *Language, Literature & Literacy in a Developing Nation*
16. *Language & Economic Reforms in Nigeria*
17. *The Syntax & Semantics of Yorùbá Nominal Expressions*
18. *Functional Categories in Igbo*
19. *Affixation and Auxiliaries in Igbo*
20. *A Grammar of Contemporary Igbo*
21. *A Concise Grammar & Lexicon of Echie*
22. *Bette Ethnography: Theory and Practice*
23. *Topical Issues in Sociolinguistics: The Nigerian Perspective*
24. *Studies in Nigerian Linguistics*
25. *Intercultural Communication & Public Policy in Nigeria*

The House of Skulls

A Symbol of Warfare & Diplomacy in Pre-Colonial Niger Delta and Igbo Hinterland

Nkparom C. Ejituwu

&

Stanley I. Okoroafor
Department of History & Diplomatic Studies
University of Port Harcourt, **Nigeria**

M & J Grand Orbit Communications Ltd
• Port Harcourt

Box 237 Uniport P.O., University of Port Harcourt,
Nigeria.
E-mail: mekuri01@yahoo.com
Mobil Phone: 08033410255, 080333589169

ISBN: 978-978-54208-5-2

Published by

M & J Grand Orbit Communications Ltd., Port Harcourt

Overseas Distributors:

African Books Collective
PO Box 721, Oxford OX1 9EN, United Kingdom
Tel: +44 (0) 1865 58 9756, Fax: +44 (0) 1865 412 341
US Tel: +1 415 644 5108

Customer Services please email
orders@africanbookscollective.com

For Warehouse/shipping/deliveries:
+44 (0) 1865 58 9756

Dedication

This book is dedicated to

My Uncle,

Ralph O. Ikuru,

for

his early interest in my education

Preface

The House of Skulls is a study of one of the lost cultures of the Niger Delta and its hinterland. The earlier draft of this book was presented as a paper at the Faculty of Humanities, University of Port Harcourt Seminar Series in 1991, where it generated much interest; some participants wanted it to be published, while others thought it would serve as evidence of African barbarity in the past. The latter view did not prevent the publication of this work now because, as will be evident in the study, some European supercargoes in the Niger Delta were far more barbaric than Africans, and their actions were so incredible that they could not be revealed and committed to this work.

The present publication of the manuscript is influenced more by "War and Peace in the Twenthieth Century", one of the National Universities Commission (NUC) history courses currently being taught by this present author at the University of Port Harcourt, Nigeria. From that course, it is evident that barbarism is not endemic to African Culture, but was part of the primitive instinct of man and the House of Skulls, as evidence of human sacrifice, and head-hunting in the Niger Delta and its hinterland in pre-colonial times was not worse than some of the practices, both African and European, which have been documented.

However, that the house of skulls is no more is not regrettable. One could look back and say: "Those were the days of African traditionalism."

I thank many people for their support and contributions to this work. Among them are: Professor Sunday Anozie of the Department of English Studies for his encouragement, Professor Robin Horton of the Department of Philosophy, Professor Emeritus E.J. Alagoa for being a "Father" to all of us, Professor Abi Derefaka, Dr. Atei M. Okorobia, Dr. Stanley I. Okoroafor for contributing a section to this book ("The Niger Delta: Its People and Cultures"), Dr. John H.

Enemugwem in helping in one way or the other, and finally Donatus O. Chuku for producing the manuscript.

I hope that the work will serve the need of scholarship, providing fresh insights into the history of one of the lost cultures of the Niger Delta, as well as instruct us that much of the culture of the Niger Delta has been modified by time.

Professor Nkparom C. Ejituwu
Professor of African History
Department of History & Diplomatic Studies
University of Port Harcourt, **Nigeria**

Table of Contents

Yok-Obolo	Obolo (Andoni) National deity
Ebeka	Kalabari National deity
Ogidiga	Nembe National deity
Fenibeso	Okrika House of Skulls
Egbesu	Nembe/Ijaw House of Skulls
Ikuba	Bonny National deity
Kamalu	Ohafia National deity
Okwuamboko	Nkoro National deity
Ibiniukpabi	Aro National deity
Okpolodo	Kalabari deity
Siri-Opubo	Kalabari deity
Ewitaraba	Obolo Thunder god
Ofiokpo	Executive Arm of Yok-Obolo
Oru	National Council of Obolo
Owemakaso	Kalabari National goddess
Peri	Chieftaincy dance
Obara-Yok	High Priest of Yok-Obolo
Nkwak	Obolo (Andoni) victory (war) dance
Okerenkwa	Ohafia victory (war) dance
YBP	Year before the present
So Alabo	High Priest of Okpolodo

Koronogbo	Kalabari Warrior Society
Oko-Yok-Obolo	Obolo (Andoni) House of Skulls

CHAPTER 1

Introduction

1.1   The House of Skulls

The House of Skulls was a European label for a house built by some Niger Delta communities with the skulls of their enemies killed in war.[1] It was so labeled by European traders, apparently, to remind themselves of their own "house of bones" which was sacred and emphasized the concern of man with the question of immortality. Emphasis on "human skulls[2] is intended to differentiate this particular "house of skulls" from "house of skulls" such as *Isi-Ebikan* of the Andoni, *Mbari* of Mbaise, *Ekpu* of Oron, and similar structures in the Niger Delta and elsewhere, which contained skulls of animals used in sacrifices, mixed with carved woods and other artifacts, designed as a memoriam of the history of the people who possessed them.

The house of skulls raises the question of

warfare and human sacrifice in pre-colonial
Niger Delta; particularly as they relate to the
attitude of the Delta people to life itself. Available
evidence indicates that warfare has been a general
feature of the delta social and economic existence.
Visiting the area in the 15th century, Pereira, a
Portuguese Captain, observed that delta people
were warlike and their belligerence affected
adversely the peace of the area.[4] Similarly, in the
17th century, probably, drawing from available
records, Dapper, a Dutch writer, stated that the
inhabitants of the Niger Delta were often at war,
selling those whom they captured into slavery,'
The story was not different in the 19th century, as
evident in Baikie's records of conflicts and wars
among the people.[6] From these records, one gets
the impression that wars among the people were
past-time and life meant nothing to them.
Evidence for this impression was the house of
skulls which stood at the centre of every major
delta city-state in the 19th century.

The reverse was the truth for wars were

fought, not as ends in themselves, but as means to specific economic and political ends. In some communities wars were fought to appease the gods of the land and/rivers and sometimes it was for plenty of harvest as the gods of their land felt happier and, in their happiness, blessed the land or river with abundant harvest and, ultimately, the people's happiness.[7] They were, in general, consequences built into the competitive search for fishing grounds in pre-colonial times: and later, as consequences of the "struggle for control" of markets or trade routes during the era of the overseas trade.[7]

The frequent references to conflicts and wars by European writers had cultural implications as well. Involved in cross-cultural setting, the European visitors to the Niger Delta were moved by the "absurd" and the "unusual," sometimes presenting these things as evidence of the barbaric nature of the African culture and yet they encouraged them as evidenced in the rise of the House of Skulls of Bonny, where they lived from the 17th century, showed.[8] Such encouragement of the growth of the House of Skulls by European traders was, indeed, a complex situation.

1.2 Development of Conflicts in the Niger Delta

Horton has identified five stages in the development of conflicts in the Niger Delta. They are as follows:

(a) Era of head-hunting and slavery;
(b) Era of fishing rights and fish traders;
(c) Era of race to the hinterland markets
   (following the arrival of European traders);
(d) Era of oil palm trade; and
(e) The era of petroleum (petro-dollars).[9]

This periodization is interesting. It takes the Niger Delta from the earliest times to the present and shows that what runs through the periods is violence. During the first two periods, life was simply uncertain in the Niger Delta as people were migrating from place to place and defence and self-preservation were necessary. For instance, when people in one canoe saw another canoe coming, they were not likely to know whether those in that canoe were friends or enemies. Therefore, defence and self preservation became the watch-word. It was only after the encounter that the people relaxed.

The third period was the time of the European slave traders. The Portuguese were the first to arrive in the Niger Delta. But whereas the products of the local people were fish and forest products, the Portuguese needed slaves.[10] The Niger Delta belonged to the Portuguese by the Treaty of Tordesillas (1494) which divided the commercial world between the Portuguese and the Spaniards." But the Portuguese had secured the *Asiento* agreement to supply the Spaniards with slaves from the Niger Delta, As such it was not surprising to see Spanish ships in the Niger Delta, collecting African slaves for their American territories for their *ecomienda* system.

Their major supply, however, was through the ports of Sao Tome in West Africa and Bahia in Brazil.[13]

The Niger Delta middlemen supplied local slaves to the European traders and when that source exhausted, they got in touch with the hinterland where there was abundant supply of slaves. This trade continued until other European nationals came in: the British, French, Dutch and others and it continued until it was stopped in the early 19th century and replaced with the palm oil trade.

Volumes could be written about the Niger Delta and palm oil trade because the problems of the trade spoke loud and clear in the direction of conflicts and the erection of the Houses of Skulls to symbolize the conflicts. However, both during the slave trade and the palm oil trade, European supercargoes showed that they were not different from the Delta middlemen. Ikime had written voluminously of the *Niger Delta Rivalry* (London, 1969). Others like K.O. Dike had written *Trade and Politics in the Niger Delta* (Oxford, 1956), G.I. Jones wrote, *The Trading States of the Oil Rivers* (Cambridge, 1963) while E.J. Alagoa wrote *A History of the Niger Delta* (Ibadan, 1972). One incident worth mentioning within the context of the Niger Delta conflict was that of "chopping of oil," and the problems arising from it."[14] "Chopping of oil" simply meant seizure of oil by one supercargo of oil belonging to another supercargo.

Niger Delta trade was based on the extension of credit by the supercargo to the Delta middleman, who then contacted his agent in the interior for oil which he would deliver to the supercargo who had advanced him the credit. But "chopping" may occur when, through pressure from another supercargo, the middleman sold the oil to another supercargo instead of the one who had advanced him the credit. Naturally, trouble arose from the "chopping" of the oil or such fraud as adulteration of the oil sold to the supercargo.

The Delta middleman delivered oil to the supercargo in casks. A cask may be a ton or more. He would half-fill the cask, more or less, with mud or any other extraneous material, and place the oil on it; and then cock it very well. This fraud would be discovered in Liverpool, the usual destination of Niger Delta oil. The Liverpool merchant would have to boil the oil until every grain of sand was removed before using it for the ultimate goal of making candles, margarine, soap, etc.

The Liverpool merchant, who was probably better in this type of fraud than the Delta middleman, would retaliate by bringing into the Niger Delta inferior goods of all types and telling the Delta people that they were the very type used by the nobility in England, etc. The Delta middleman who had no choice would parade this false information, in the Delta and in the hinterland as correct, and fraud would go on indefinitely. This was the scenario that gave Dike the basis of describing the palm oil traders -both white and black – as "palm oil ruffians." The palm oil ruffians generated disputes of all kinds; sometimes leading to shootout in the Niger Delta with disastrous consequences.

One of the byproducts of this was the establishment of the Court of Equity by the British in Bonny and elsewhere in the Niger Delta to settle disputes between Delta middlemen and European supercargoes. A simple example was the one described as "diplomacy" by Comte C.N. de Cardi.[16] When a Niger Delta middleman told a "lie," he was regarded as having "lied". But when a European supercargo told a "lie," he was regarded as being "diplomatic."[17] This double-standard created so much difficulty which the British Government tried to resolve through the setting up of the Court of Equity; a kind of International Court of Justice, to settle disputes in the region.

In their interest to get in touch with the

hinterland, the British established the ports of Port Harcourt in the Eastern Delta and Warri in the Western Niger Delta and indirectly forced the Niger Delta middlemen to go there for trade and businesses.[18]

Finally, the last stage, namely, the era of petroleum industry. Niger Delta, apparently, "refused" to dry up of resources." It kept yielding resources of all kinds and attracting migrants from everywhere for resource exploitation. By the end of the 19th century, the British had colonized the Niger Delta, calling it "Nigeria."[19] In 1956 crude oil was discovered in the Niger Delta and exploitation began almost immediately. Along with the exploitation came several international companies into the Niger Delta to exploit it: Shell, Agip, American Chevron, Mobil, Willbros, Schlumberger, Halliburton, etc. came into the Niger Delta to exploit the crude oil. Crude oil was being bought in dollars and profit was enormous. On the contrary, exploitation of the oil has left the Niger Delta region environmentally poor, and the cries of the people of marginalization of the area has not changed anything. Out of this scenario, there emerged a group of youths who called themselves "Militants;" and who engaged in the kidnapping, first of "oil workers," who were mostly white, and when "whitemen" were no longer available for kidnapping, they went over to prosperous local men and women with kidnap value. Such persons include those with potential resource base for ransom money.[20]

Analysis of the comparative eras shows that the major common factor running through the entire periods was violence. It ran from the beginning of the pre-colonial times to the modern times. However, the activities of the militants are so special that we cannot accommodate them in this study to enable us focus on the House of Skulls and its allied problems of twin-killing, human sacrifice and similar practices which made the supercargoes respect and encourage its growth.

1.3 The Hinterland

Because of the fact that the competing Delta political entities depended on the immediate hinterland for goods and foodstuffs for sale to European traders, the study also extends to the hinterland areas such as Arochukwu, Ndoki, Oguta, Ohafia and others who are known to have practiced head-hunting.[21] So, the aim of this study is to trace the origin, function, and collapse of the House of Skulls, not only in the Niger Delta, but also in these hinterland areas.

Some emphasis will also be placed on the variations in the use of the cult in the various places where it was practiced for such variations would indicate the dynamism of the institution as well as provide insights into the function and direction of the spread.

Notes

1. Nkparom C. Ejituwu, "Warfare and Diplomacy in the Niger Delta" in *Warfare and Diplomacy in Pre-Colonial Nigeria* (eds.) Toyin Falola and Robin Law (Madison: University of Wisconsin Press, 1992), pp.199-207. Also, Kay Williamson, "Linguistic Evidence for the Pre-History of the Niger Delta" in E J. Alagoa, F. Anozie and N. Nzewunwa (eds.), *The Early History of the Niger Delta* (Hamburg, 1985), pp. 65-179.

2. Professor William Feuser of the Department of Foreign Languages, University of Port Harcourt, in a personal communication, 13 June, 1992. Also, E.J. Alagoa, *A History of the Niger Delta*, (Ibadan, 1992), p.154.

3. Philip O. Nsugbe, "Oron Ekpu Figures," *Nigeria Magazine*, 71 (1961), pp. 357-359.

4. GHT. Kimble (trans.), *Esmeraldo de Situ Orbis* (London, 1937), p. 132.

5. Olfert   Dapper,   *Description   of   Africa* (Amsterdam, 1668).

6. William Baikie, *Narrative of an Exploring Voyage* (London, 1856).

7. Sunny Abel Dickay, "War and Symbols of War in Obukegi (Ogba-Egbema-Ndoni LGA)." (University of Port Harcourt, 1999).

8. E.J. Alagoa, *A History of the Niger Delta* (Ibadan, 1972). Robin Horton in a personal communication, University of Port Harcourt, 1999.

9. GHT. Kimble, (Trans.) *Esmeraldo de Situ Orbis* (London, 1937), p. 132.

10. J.H. Parry, *Europe and the Wider World* (Ibadan, 1964).

11. *Ibid.*

12. *Ibid.* Also, see Nkparom C. Ejituwu, "Old Calabar Rediscovered," (University of Lagos Press, 1999), pp 133-150.

13. K.O. Dike, *Trade and Politics in the Niger Delta* (Oxford, 1956). pp. 109-110.

14. *Ibid.*

15. Comte C.N. de Cardi, "A Short Description of the Natives of the Coast Protectorate" in Mary Kingsley, *West African Studies* (London, 1899), pp. 443-556.
16. *Ibid.*
17. G.I. Jones, *The Trading States of the Oil Rivers* (Cambridge, 1963). Port Harcourt also owed its foundation to the discovery of coal in Enugu in 1913, and the need for its export overseas.
18. G.I. Jones, *The Trading States of the Oil Rivers* (Cambridge, 1963).
19. Alan Burns, *A History of Nigeria* (London, 1978).
20. Nnah B. Barinem, "Towards a Holistic Peace Process for the Niger Delta" (MA Thesis, University of Port Harcourt, 2008). Protest of marginalization and under-development of the region. Two notable militant groups are Niger Delta People's Volunteer Force led by Mujahid Asari Dokubo and Niger Delta Vigilante led by Ateke Tom. These are the prominent ones among other smaller militias, numbering up to 100 or more. They use Rocket Propelled Grenades, AK-47s, Machine Guns,

Satellite Phones and Speed Boats. E. Cesarz, J.S. Morisou and Cooke, *Alienation and Militancy in Nigeria's Niger Delta* (CSIS Africa Notes, No. 16, May Centre for Strategic and International Studies. Washington, DC).

21. William Baikie. *Narrative of an Exploring Voyage*, London, 1856).

CHAPTER 2

The Niger Delta: Its People & Cultures

2.1 The Niger Delta

The Niger Delta is the region served by the Niger River and stretches from the Escravos in the west to the Cross River in the East. The Niger River rises from the Kukuruku Hills and Futa Jallon mountains in Sierra Leone region of West Africa and, running East and then South, joins the Benue River which rises from the Adamawa mountains in the Nigeria-Cameroon border and runs South. The two rivers merged at Lokoja and formed a formidable body of water which empties into the Atlantic Ocean. Before emptying into the Atlantic Ocean, it segments into a series of creeks and rivulets and ultimately the swamps called the Niger Delta.[1]

The debris brought from a thousand-mile journey was deposited in the creeks and rivers where it served as nutrients for fish and other aquatic life, with great implications for human migrations into the Niger Delta. The aquatic animals (planktons) deposited in the area over the millennia converted into the crude oil (petroleum) now abundant in the area.[2]

Over the crude oil and materials stood the vegetation of mangrove swamps which Mary Kingsley, the British explorer of the 19th century, described as one of the greatest in the world.[3] According to her, "the swamp of [the Niger Delta] is the greatest in the World and, in its immensity and gloom, it has a grandeur equal to the Himalayas,[4] South of the Niger Delta is the Gulf of Guinea which borders on the Atlantic Ocean.

2.2 The Peopling of the Niger Delta

A comprehensive look at the peopling of the Niger Delta would take a longer discussion to be properly captured. Therefore, such a succinct presentation as is desired in this piece would only serve as highlights of the actual exposition.

Today, the Niger Delta enjoys a lot of patronage

so much so that the entire population of southern Nigeria is affiliated and associated to it. Some of these are Edo, Itsekiri, Urhobo, Ishan, Isoko, Igbo, Ijo, Ogoni, Obolo (Andoni), Ekpeye, Ogba, Okrika, Kalabari, Efik, Ibibio, Nkoro, Ikwerre, Oru, Abua and Okpe. This is because an understanding of the land and the people therein would have nine states (namely: Ondo, Edo, Delta, Bayelsa, Imo, Abia, Akwa Ibom and Rivers) of today's Nigeria, forming the Niger Delta states.[5] This notwithstanding, it is also understood that only some parts of some of these states are really of the Niger Delta and also the people in them. This has made some people to think of some area of the region as being the core area (e.g. Bayelsa, Rivers and Delta States) and others, the peripheries, This understanding is appreciated but does not make a part of the people there more of the Delta than the other(s). There is rather an attempt to see them as one with common environmental experience following the manners of settlement and after- settlement developments that have come to shape and reshape the historical situations of land

and people of the Delta.

Nonetheless the main population group of the delta is the Ijo (the Ijoid groups)[6]. The Ijo people are diversely situated in the Delta and can be found in most of the region's states. They appear to have been in the core delta before many others and have mastered the terrain, adapting quite well in it. The Ijo, however, may not have been to all the areas they are found today before the people inhabiting the areas. They had in the main by-passed some ethnic groups to be where they are today and had in their nomadic manner moved to many other areas in search of more fleshy waters.

The Delta had been populated as the land emerged from under the waters (of the sea and the mirage of rivers and other waters of the Niger). As such earlier occupants of the areas of the Niger Delta especially to the North and the fringes had arrived and settled earlier than when the Ijo people arrived the Delta. It is known now from findings that almost the entire people of the Niger Delta are of the Kwa language family of Congo-

Kordofanian which split up into many languages about seven thousand years ago. Experts have also shown the direction of the coming of the Ijo people to be from the North Central area of Nigeria (that is the middle belt around the confluent area of Rivers Niger and Benue).[7]

Talbot (1932) had thought so and had seen Ijo people as a group on the run in the distant time whose distinct language from other ethnic groups around the delta indicates that they have lived for a long time in the region, Alagoa and Derefaka (1988:6) disclosed that the notion of the ancestral proto - Ijo speakers having come down the River Niger is merely a vague suggestion by some like Talbot [8]. This argument seems to hold water but also makes one see the possibility or otherwise of the central Niger Delta, being the place of earliest settlement and dispersal of the people. It was this kind of supposition, sometimes backed by some oral information that warranted the prehistoric search of the origin and dispersal of Ijo people within the Delta to being at the central Niger Delta.

However, with some geomorphological information on the region's land development, and subsequent peopling, the central Niger Delta area would have been one of the last places in the delta to get dried up and allow human habitation. This is because, it is in it that the Niger's central and fallout water courses, flow into the sea. From the excavation of Nzewunwa in Ogba land and the core bore at Ofuabo creek near Nembe and studied by Sowunmi, it is evident that land had emerged within the vertical stretch of the delta 3,000 YBP.[5]

A look at the peopling of the Niger Delta would present three ideas about how the people of the region came to be, namely, the autochthonous, the emigrants and the fusions. For the autochthonous group, there is not much of conviction about the position taken by such group since the Niger Delta is relatively young in its formation and settlement by man. Sometimes such groups account about their coming and settling in the area could be trapped by things like myths, and unable to decode such, the people would think of themselves as having come from nowhere outside where they are found.

For the second viewpoint, which makes more sense, given the geological and general environmental understanding of the region, it seems that the Niger was the main course through which the various population clusters found, came to be in it and from there, later developments in the general settlement pattern of the people. With regard to this development, there had been steady movement of the populations and crisis-crossing of the area of many groups at different times. It became more intricate, given that particular groups of people move say eastwards, then go westward subsequently and later return to settle to the east, about where they had been before; staying in each place as long as they deemed good. This has been supported by some of the oral accounts on the people's origin and migration.

The third viewpoint is another possibility in the sense that both the cultural and linguistic evidence bear witness to such development in the Niger

Delta. Horton had captured this notion with 'ama' example between the Obolo (Andoni) group and the Ijo people, used together, meaning the same, indicating fusion (acculturation and assimilation) of both.[10]. Here though, Horton needed to see beyond both parties and to observe that most people of South-east and South-south Nigeria use the same word to mean the same (town) or about the same (street, open playground). In virtually all comers (Oguta, Ogbakiri, Nembe, Degema, Kula, etc.) of the deltas, there had been such development. These understandings are there in the delta but the issues and problems begging for clarification from researchers have been when such immigrations or fusions happened and how they occurred. These have been made more intricate with the new wave of politicking and adaptation.

The main stream of Ijo migration account makes it clear that Aboh was already in existence where they are today before the Ijo group moved over to the delta to stay. Aboh is one of the peoples of the delta northern fringe, the 'head', who had maintained that their earlier place of sojourn was among the defunct Benin kingdom and who; for some political troubles, emigrated into the places where they are found today from about the 15th C. Both Aboh and Oguta to the 'Head' of the delta have accounts of harbouring some of the later emigrants into the delta (See Ellah 1995). The Edo people themselves had gone into the delta just before the dusk of the first millennium from some place north of their present homeland. The Itsekiri who were a part of this early development had just like the Ijo, gone deeper into the delta to the west to stay. The Urhobo and their Okpe and Isoko relations also became part of the delta population at about this time. There has not been any archaeological excavation to hold strong some of the cases made in some earlier reconstructions in this regard. Such blessing has been received mainly by the broad eastern side of the delta. Here, starting from the central Niger Delta to the eastern, northern delta and their fringes, archaeological works have aided in the fuller and more authentic understanding of the origins of the people in these areas of the delta. There has been, for example, a clearer picture of the constitution of the population clusters. As such, one can see how they are, in their cultural diversity, related and associated. From such, for example, one can make out some indisputable facts about them and still some conjectures.

The entire people, it is clear, came from the northern directions through diverse routes. Sometimes they zigzagged areas of the delta before finally settling where they are today. Most of them point at Benin as one place which they came from but some of such as simply claims arising from wanting to be associated with a celebrated success point, or perhaps to be reckoned with and not be bullied by others around. Experts have discountenanced some of such, due to lack of concrete fact connecting some to the then Benin people and their glorious kingdom. In another vein, some would for social-political reasons want to be associated with the dominant population group in the delta (in this case the Ijo) seeking protection and a balance of the nation's social-political equation. For instance, recently a researcher thought that he was right, seeing the people of Akwete as Ijo people.

Even when we know that some of the earliest radio carbon dates obtained from the eastern side came from the Ijoid population, for example, Ke and Okochiri, it is still not enough to determine who arrived first or the direction of their coming. The Obolo (Andoni) people seem to have arrived early in time even before most of the people in the delta although this cannot be substantiated in the mean time. Obolo (Andoni) tradition, historically woven, has it that they came from the Nile area around East Africa and had gone to the famous Benin kingdom (there is no clear evidence to justify this claim), from where they entered into the delta. This interesting people of the delta may hold the key to our proper understanding of the peopling of the area since they have things to do with virtually every ethnic group in the delta from the Itsekiri to the Edo, the Igbo, Ijo, Efik, Ibibio and the Ibani and Okrika. The supposition in the pattern of migration has been that most of the people of the eastern part of the delta had passed through the Niger. This may not be the case for every one of them. The Niger had many countries or its sides from the Igala land-Agenebode axis, to the place of its bifurcation at Omoku. In these countries and the city-states were authorities and suzerainties that would not compromise steady influx of population that could become a threat to them sooner or later. Some people had passed through it successfully but others were just not allowed. Oguta, for example, had moved to where they are today against such formidable groups like Aboh and Illah, about when Oba Esigie's trouble in Benin was intense.

It makes sense to think that some of the people had passed through smaller rivers flanking the Niger, which served the same purpose, with minimal obstruction, as was the case of the Niger. Ase River to the left, Cross and Imo Rivers to the east of the Niger would have presented alternate routes to go through and enter into the delta. Oguta and some Ekpeye groups did so as had been revealed through the oral traditions of the peoples. Oguta was already familiar with water life and did not have much problems taking through the waters to arrive in their homeland. Again, some of such smaller rivers were shallower and fordable.

The Ibibio people are another interesting people of the Niger Delta today, Scholars almost unanimously point at the Cameroon as their place of origin, from where they came to the Niger Delta. Talbot (1926), suggests a date of about 9000 JBP as the beginning time of the people. When they entered the Niger Delta area is not really known. However, they appear to have adapted quite well in their domains that they seem to have stayed in it for a long time. Knowledge of the Niger Delta history nonetheless begins also with the advent of the European as from about 1472 A.D.

The Efik people are the closest relation of the

Ibibio people. They too, like the Ibibio, are said to have come from the Cameroon, and had lived amongst the Igbo and migrated because they did not want to be oppressed. The time of their coming to their present homeland is said to be after the 15th century since both the Bonny and Kalabari peoples who are also of the Niger Delta settled in it in the late 15th century. They had met on arrival from the east of their homeland today, the Qua, the Efut and the Abakpa peoples. There must have been assimilation and acculturation and for some, there are homogeneities in language and culture between them and the earlier occupants of the land. For it is factual that the way the peoples (Efik and Ibibio) are today is but a fallout of the clans[1] groups distribution which has been informed by a "wide variety and types of movement which date to well beyond the 15th century".

From Horton's (1998) good work on the eastern Ijo origins and expansion, one can deduce that the Ijoid group, perhaps, came through the east of the delta and had gone westward into their other homelands today. Or moreso that after they arrived via that eastern direction, that the other Ijo folks moved in from the central direction most likely through the river Niger and some other adjacent rivers to the Niger such as west of the Niger. Horton had pictured the scenario when Obolo (Andoni) settled long before the coming of the Ijo groups. Some Ijo population that came after the Andoni, clusters around the Obolo (Andoni) people. Tradition of origin informed us that such communities are the Alabie, Asarama and Ilotombi which are all of Ijo stock. They settled around 1500 JDP after the original Obolo people had settled. This establishes the fact that some of the Obolo (Andoni) are of Ijo stock. The earliest writer on the people of the Niger Delta, Pereira Pacheco, had written of the people he met about 1500 AD as Ijo (or Jos). The Portuguese met a large village, such being the identity of the population clusters of the negroids found between the estuary of the Forcados to the west and the Rio Real to the eastern fringe of the delta. This though was done at the southern end of the delta but not dealing with the entire delta. Moreover, there had been migrations and emigration out of and into areas of the Delta before this time, of different peoples, such as can be found today.

Although there had been archaeological excavation in Okochiri and Ogoloma of Okrika, the results are full of unresolved issues. First, of which is where the people came from. Is it the 'Brass' area westward in the Central Niger Delta or the Obolo (Andoni) river to the eastern fringe of the delta? Second, who among Oputibeya and Kirike first settled in the place and welcomed the other in the same land? However, the Okrika confederation is a mixture of Obolo (Andoni) and Ijoid groups.

Ndoki people, an Igboid group are an example of such people of the Niger Delta who have had very close association with the Obolo (Andoni) and Ijoid groups to the coast for quite sometime that there has come to be well emphasized acculturation in names and certain aspects of their behaviour. The Akwete weaving tradition is an example of such relationship. On the cloth can be found the imprints of the world view *(Ikakibite)* of some of such coastal dwellers of the delta but woven in by these contractors who should do the wish of their clients to keep up with the business. Whereas there had been debates on the routes through which some Niger Delta people (example the Ijo) came into the delta, such has not been the case with others, especially those at the periphery of the delta. The Ijo people were said to have come in through the apex. This is contestable, given the result of some of the historical researches carried out thus far in the area concerning the people's origin, emigration and settlement. Coming through the apex would translate to coming through the River Niger. The position here is that all the Ijo people did not come at the same time or and, perhaps, had had alternate routes especially via such rivers besides the Niger.

This view is supported by the linguistic evidence of the origin of the people and their dispersal and settlement. Going by such evidence, proto Ijoid people like the original Obolo (Andoni) arrived the delta from the eastern direction. Also they were part of the disintegrating and expanding Niger-Congo which is a sub-branch of a larger Niger-Saharan phylum that is linked with the Nilo-Saharan (the homeland of Niger-Congo has been located east of Lake Chad as, cited in (Horton 1998). These views, though Horton would think have linguistic lapses, are most plausible, given the fact that such present more logical reasoning.

The Ogoni claim to have come from Ghana. This is similar to some Efik tradition of origin, which also point at Ghana as the place of their original homeland.[24] These fall into the emigrant group but which do not have any strong evidence backing them up either in the form of linguistic data or cultural materials.

Peopling of the Niger Delta is observed to have been complex in nature, having turned out gradually and intricately. The people, in broad terms, are homogeneous, being in all, of the Kwa language family and a Negroid people. The complexity of the origin of the people, the migrations and settlements, make it more than the work of the historian to deal with but those of linguists, anthropologists, ethnographers, art historians and, more important- ly, archaeologists. Much of the reconstruction using, historical, linguistic and ethnographic data and paradigms of interpretation has been done with some rewards. It is hoped that when new and more scientific methods are used such as geomorphology and archaeology, clearer results would be secured, with which more vivid reconstruction and interpretation would be done on the understanding of the peoples of the Niger Delta. Such is necessary in the growth and development of the region and the nation at large. The rate of social economic and environmental degradation in the area stems more from the poor understanding of the area by everybody dealing with it and should be looked into and stopped.

However, as said earlier, some of the people who had migrated and inhabited the area are the Ijo, Obolo (Andoni), Kalabari, Nembe-Brass, Okrika,

Itsekiri, Bonny, Bille, Ohafia and others. Of all these people, the Ijo are the most dominant inhabitants of the area. For a long time, their origin was shrouded in mystery. But now it is being suggested that, like the Niger River, the Ijo may have originated from the hinterland and, following the Niger River and the Benue River, found themselves in the Niger Delta.

2.3   The People and their Cultures
Culture is indispensably necessary; and culture is the totality of a people's inventions (material and immaterial) to enable them to control their individual environments for survival. In this case, the environment is the Niger Delta and its hinterland.

Basic to Niger Delta people was the fishing economy and around the fishing there developed various practices, essential to the survival and expansion of the economy. The canoe, for instance, is basic and has been compared, in importance, to the camel in the Sahara desert. Movement from one village to the other in the Niger Delta could only be done by canoe. So was marine warfare and military manoeuvres. The canoe was indispensable.

Drumming was essential to *the* life of the people. It elevated the spirit and made life worth living in the watery environment of the Niger Delta. Wrestling has been reported as the inevitable past-time of the people.

Religion is a major issue and is a function of the very turbulent nature of the area. Thus, each village or group has its god and priesthood attached to it. The god and its priesthood must be appeased through prayers and offerings of goods. Some of the gods are war-gods and demanded not only animal but also human offerings. Human sacrifice and warfare were foundations of the House of Skulls.

2.4 Focus on the Obolo (Andoni)

This section derives from certain references made of Obolo (Andoni) in terms of the peopling of the Eastern Delta. For instance, Anene, in his book *Southern Nigeria in Transition* (London, 1966), said that before the Ijo of the Central Delta got to the Eastern Delta, the Obolo (Andoni) were already settled[25]. Then, Alagoa mentioned the peregrination of the Ijo in the Central Delta.[26] Those Ijo who left the Central Delta for the Eastern Delta also confirmed the primacy of the Obolo (Andoni) in the Eastern Delta. E.D.W. Opu-Ogulaya of Okrika was very specific. He said that by the time the Ijo got to the Eastern Delta, the Obolo (Andoni) were already *in situ*. They were the ones controlling the Big River, which the Ijo called *Idontoro*, meaning, the "Andoni River."[27]

As we will see in this work, Tonye V. Erekosima will credit the Obolo (Andoni) as being the people first met by the Portuguese traders when they came to the Eastern Delta in the 15th century.[28] The "Big River" of the Ijo was the River the Portuguese called "Rio Real," the largest river in the Eastern Niger Delta. It had a village of some 2,000 inhabitants located on it in a creek which research will probably identify as Asarama. Asarama was later removed by competition with other villages when the overseas trade became fierce and very competitive.[29]

This is not all. Professor Williamson and Professor Horton will similarly speak of the Obolo (Andoni) as the centre of trade and activities. And because of these references, there is need to focus on the Obolo (Andoni), using the information available to reconstruct a history of the people with respect to the place and activities of the people.

Many of the Ijo speaking peoples targeted, the "Big River" which the Obolo (Andoni) called *Okwuan Obolo* meaning, "Andoni River." Incidentally, the Obolo (Andoni) and their King exercised control over the river. Because of the size of the river, certain very large fishes were caught in it and such fishes were not to be eaten privately by the catchers: they were to be handed over to the King of Obolo (Andoni) for public functions[31]. Such fishes included *inan* (giant groupers), *ikurumun* (giant turtles), *nririen* (manatees), etc.

Some of the Ijo who arrived in the area to live

with the Obolo (Andoni) and fish in the river did not like some of these laws because, according to them, the laws were degrading and they had to migrate further. Among these were the founders of Ogoloma, Bolo and Ogu.[32]

The Obolo (Andoni) did not only have rivers to control. They also have thick forests and "flat" lands. The so-called "Andoni Mainland," running from Oyorokoto in the west to Down-bellow in the east, is a fertile land with all kinds of wild animals. In this forest are to be found elephants, pythons, leopards, wild-pigs, swamp crocodiles and all kinds of birds. Since the colonial days, efforts were made to convert the jungle into a Games Reserve or Tourist Attraction Site. But Government after Government had failed to do so probably because of the huge cost the project would entail. South of this land is the Atlantic Ocean [32].

There is also the "Andoni Flat" which Professor S.J.S. Cookey called "a Natural Fish Pond." That is because when water ebbs, it is pure flat land (mud). But when water flows, it is an "ocean" of water.[34] It is simply beautiful! Before the beginning of the petroleum industry, fish was abundant in the "Andoni Flat." The Obolo (Andoni) controlled these places and influenced fishing and life of people coming in for the exploitation of the resources of the Rivers.

It is not surprising that many of such people speak of having to leave the area because of the stringent rules made by the King of Andoni. As we said earlier, the Okrika, Ogoloma, Bolo, Ogu, Ohafia and others had to leave the *Idontoro* to where they are now because of these laws and the pressures of the Obolo (Andoni) on the people.

The Ohafia, who called themselves *Mbem Owan*, lived with the Andoni at Okwala, and were professional head-hunters. Apparently, they also fished, traded and did other petty businesses in Andoni until the arrival of the Portuguese when their interests clashed with those of the Andoni and the Portuguese; and they had to leave the Eastern Niger Delta for the hinterland. The Ohafia presence in Obolo (Andoni) and subsequent migration into the hinterland will be discussed further.

The House of Skulls symbolized the Andoni political and military dominance in the area. This requires a specific mention of the people in military and political terms.

At the apex of the Andoni political and military structure was *Yok-Obolo*, the people's national deity. Next to him was *Ewitaraba*, the god of Thunder, symbolized by the Ram and described by Leonard as similar, in function, to *Sango*, the Yoruba god of Thunder.[35] On the human level were the High Priest and the King who administered to the deity. These were supported by *Oru*, a Council of State (the legislature and judiciary) and *Ofiokpo*, a select group of freeborn, which was responsible for a tribute system. Below the King and the High Priest were the common people who paid annual taxes in the form of tribute. There were about twenty-one villages at this time; and taxes collected from each of the villages were divided into two halves, one half being retained in the village for the maintenance of the village shrine while the other half went to Dony

Town, the capital, for the maintenance of the High Priest, burial of the dead and support of warfare. All the proceeds from the tribute system were housed in the *Oko-Yok-Obolo* House of Skulls with a special family *(Agwut Ubong)*, placed over it as the caretaker. The family head was the Andoni national treasurer.

The structure was supported by a social system and a military machine which, they claimed, was second to none in the Niger Delta. The idea is that *Yok-Obolo*, the national deity, placed a great value on every living Andoni because, according to the tradition, the latter was the deity's soldier. For this, a census of the national population was a regular feature of the Andoni political system. Thus, when an Andoni was dead, his/her body was brought before the deity for the necessary rituals, and, if it was a female of advanced age, a large quantity *of alata* (bronzes) was given out from the central purse for burial along with the body. Men were given national burial but were not decorated like women.

If an Andoni was dead or missing and he/she was found to have been slain by another Andoni, the latter was tried and, if found guilty, was summarily executed at *Ichiama*, a place reserved for such purpose. If the man had been slain by a non-Andoni person, *Yok-Obolo*, would insist on replacement; which meant that the person responsible for the death or someone else from his community, would be killed and the head brought to the House of Skulls for keep.

Yok-Obolo was a god of war. But, he did not allow indiscriminate warfare. Thus, it was often very difficult to get permission from him to go to war against an external enemy. But once permission was given, the war must be fought and trophies in the form of human heads presented to him. As part of the tradition, women must not be killed in war unless they were armed and threatening. Men who returned from the battle-field with trophies in the form of human heads were decorated with eagle plumes and allowed to enjoy certain privileges in the society, privileges such as being able to drink palm wine with the left hand in a gathering of equals. There is no indication that such persons formed a class in the society as we would see elsewhere.

Barbot saw some of these things when he visited the people in 1699. Apart from the King, whom he described as a good natured man, who spoke the Portuguese language fluently and seemed to have been Christianized by the Portuguese, he also saw the High Priest whom he called *Marabou*. The latter was "highly respected" by the common people who were "circumcised." Iguana (*Varanus miloticus*) was revered as part of the cult of the House of Skulls; and any person who touched any of these things with his hands was sure to be severely punished, and in danger of losing his life.

These observations seem to be evidence that, up to that time, the Andoni were a military force. Fombo was later to say:

Of wars with Kalabari, Ogoni, the hinterland and other peoples, the Ibani man will talk lightly. But he will never talk lightly when Andoni wars were mentioned.[36]

In an age when warfare and bravery meant political and economic success, the example of the Obolo (Andoni) was admired by the surrounding peoples.

2.5 The Arrival of the Portuguese Traders

The first European trader of significance to visit the Eastern Niger Delta was Duarte Pachecco Pereira. He was a Portuguese sailor who visited the area in about 1485 and traded with Delta people. In his book, *Esmeraldo de Situ Orbis* (trans.) G.H.T. Kimble (London, 1937), he discussed trade in the Delta. First, he mentioned the Rio Real, the largest river in the Eastern Delta, on which there was a large village with some 2,000 inhabitants located in the creek. And people in large canoes came from up the river to trade with the village. The articles of trade included sheep, palm oil, yams, etc.

This information indicates that before the

initiation of the overseas trade, there was an internal trade between Delta people and the hinterland and that the overseas trade was only grafted to an existing trade. The overseas trade revolutionized the trade of the Niger Delta.

According to Tonye Erekosima, when the Portuguese came to the Niger Delta, they first met the Andoni people.[37] Also, the Andoni were the first to gain ascendancy in this new trade for which the Europeans freely supplied them with guns, rums, etc., to encourage them to raid on other local people. Other communities like Bonny, Kalabari, Okrika, Nembe, etc., got into the new trade in the spirit of intense competition and military rivalry and the war-canoes became a veritable trading cooperation with self-development capabilities in which personal activities became the intense competition and brutal rivalry. What Erekosima is saying is, indeed, a reflection of the major issue in Europe, with a spill-over into the Niger Delta.

The Portuguese had got to India and, as a result, a considerable quantity of spices and wealth was flowing into Portugal. Similarly, the Spaniards got to America and gold and silver were flowing into Spain. To ensure peace between them, the Treaty of Tordesillas (1494) was made to divide the World between Spain and Portugal and while Portugal got the East, Spain got the West. Pope Alexander VI divided the commercial world into two halves between Portugal and Spain[38]. In so doing, he had behaved as if the other European nations would not be interested in the commercial expansion. Soon, they entered the trade in the spirit of rivalry and broke the Spanish and Portuguese monopoly of the world trade. The theatre of their rivalry was the Niger Delta. The Portuguese were in Andoni, the British in Bonny, the Dutch in New Kalabari (New Calabar), the French in Nembe-Brass and the Niger Delta rivalry had begun. As said earlier, the major writers on the Niger Delta trade, including T.V. Erekosima, had written of the Niger Delta rivalry.

The Andoni who had the upper hand in the trade, lost it to Bonny and Kalabari, etc. All Delta city states made contacts with the hinterland for slaves and later for palm oil and the Niger Delta rivalry was in vogue.

This clear cut division of the city-states between the Europeans is not totally correct. For instance, although Dony Town belonged to the Portuguese, by trade, the British and the Dutch also traded there. In 1868 the French, Comte C.N. de Cardi, traded in Dony Town as well as in Brass.[16] As we saw already, Barbot was there in 1699 and he traded comfortably.

2.6 Warfare and Diplomacy

Niger Delta people had been engaging in warfare and diplomacy long before the arrival of the European traders. The arrival of the European traders, however, revolutionized warfare and diplomacy in that it shifted traditional warfare from the "limited" to the "large" scale. A brief demonstration of this will illustrate the point.

A village wakes up one morning to find that one or two of its girls had disappeared. Inquiries soon show that the two girls had been kidnapped by persons from a neighbouring village. The leaders of the village would put in motion the necessary diplomatic moves. First, they would send to the other village a piece of "yam" and an "arrow" or a "spear," with an instruction to them to choose peace or war.[39] Among the Ikwerre, it was two pieces of sticks, one dry and the other fresh, the dry stick symbolizing war;[40] while, among the Etche, it was "chalk" and a "bullet," the bullet symbolizing war.[41]

The symbols were traditional and were fully understood. If the leaders of the second village chose "yam", peace would be reached very easily. The leaders of the first village would get back their girls or compromise their losses and normal relationship would resume. On the other hand, if the second village chose the "spear," both sides would begin to prepare for war. If the village that was offended defeated the second village, the concept of "limited" warfare would apply in the sense that the victor may kill one or two warriors and expect the two girls to be returned or replaced as part of the settlement. At the end the damage was minimal. That was the concept of "limited" warfare practiced by Africans in pre-colonial time. The concept of limited warfare made for environmental replenishment and ecological balance.

The arrival of European traders changed the traditional system of warfare and diplomacy from the limited to the large scale invasion and large scale killing. King Jaja's invasion of Ibeno (1881) was an example of this new method; and Nembe's invasion of the Royal Niger factories at Akassa (1895) was another.[43] The symbols also changed from "yam" and "spear" to "Bible" and "Cannon Ball" and later "Gunboat." All these not only led to large scale destruction, but also to a higher frequency of wars to keep the items of trade: slaves, palm oil, etc, flowing.

Another factor in the Niger Delta warfare and diplomacy was the "alliance system." We have already indicated that Europeans entered world trade in the spirit of rivalry with Portugal and Spain and bequeathed part of this rivalry to the Niger Delta when the latter became a theatre of the trade.

The European traders succeeded in finding

bases at various places in the Delta: We have already seen that the Portuguese were friends of the Obolo (Andoni). Later the English, Dutch, French and others came in with larger vessels and found deeper waters in other places in the Niger Delta. The English were in Bonny, the Dutch in New Calabar, the French in Brass and so on. These associations were not fixed as the European traders' movements could be flexible. The English, for instance, based in Bonny, but they contacted Obolo (Andoni) and New Calabar with "Long boats" and "Pinnacles."[*1] The French were in Brass, but they could trade in Obolo (Andoni) as well. In 1704 John Grazilhier, a Dutch trader, hunted elephants with the King of Obolo (Andoni), using all kinds of weapons in the process. In this way, the European traders influenced the trade of the Niger Delta.

The trade of the Niger Delta was conducted in such a way that war and peace were built into the structure of the trade. For instance, a community may host a group of European traders because of their deep seaport, but they had no control of the trade route to the hinterland markets. And so, if the host community brutalized their neighbours, such neighbours retaliated when an opportunity occurred for the offenders to pass through their territory to the hinterland markets. In this way, the Niger Delta trade became lively, whether it was during the slave trade, palm oil trade or petroleum trade and war and peace were made integral part of the structure of the trade.

Sometimes, Niger Delta city-states allied with one another in actual conflicts and battles. In 1828 Bonny allied with Ogoni against the Obolo village of Unyeada. In 1846 Okrika allied with Obolo (Andoni) against Bonny. On another time, Nembe and Okrika allied against Kalabari.[45] In this way, the Niger Delta states acted as Europeans when they formed alliances and fought one another for economic and political reasons.

Like Europeans also, they changed sides when the object of their combination changed. In the western Niger Delta, the story was the same as the city-states there formed alliances and fought for economic and political gains very much like those in the Eastern Delta.

2.7 The Hinterland

The immediate hinterland of the Eastern Niger Delta is inhabited by the Ogoni, Ibibio, Ikwerre and Igbo while the Western Delta is inhabited by the Urhobo, Isoko, Ukwani and others. The main feature of these areas is thick forests in some parts and arable land in the others. Thus, they produced tools and forest products for nutrition, Because of the predominantly fish-and-salt mono culture of the Delta, a symbolic existence exists between the Delta and its hinterland. For instance, short and long distance trade developed between the delta and the hinterland as the latter provided most of the foodstuffs consumed in the Delta as well as sold to European traders when the overseas trade started in the 15th century. So there was a constant North-South-North movement of peoples and vice versa. Equally, there was movement across the

Delta. It has been said that a canoe can take off from Lagos Lagoon, and without coming out into the open sea, reach the Cross River in the East.

The geographical arrangement also created conditions for war and peace since traders had to travel long distances to well-known markets and fairs and the death of a member often attracted revenge from the community from which the victim had come. Pereira, visiting the Niger Delta at the end of the 15th century, recorded the existence of this long-distance trade when he observed that men from over a hundred leagues upstream came in canoe to trade with a village in the Delta with some 2,000 people. He also recorded that Delta people were rarely at peace since they carried daggers like those of the White Moors of Barbery and fought and defended themselves with them.

2.8 Conclusion

We have seen the Niger Delta and its people. We have noted that the Niger Delta is watered by the

Niger River that flows from the interior. This river created the Niger Delta with abundant resources which have been a source of attraction for people in the hinterland and elsewhere.

Among the people visiting the Niger Delta are European traders. Such visits started from about the 15th century and grew with passing years. Because of the diverse interests of the people and the abundant resources available for exploitation, violence became a constant factor in the relationship. The symbol of that violence was the House of Skulls that stood in the centre of every city-state and reminded visitors of the need to behave because of the power and strength of their host communities.

The question that remains to be answered now is what was the origin(s) of the House of Skulls, its functions, and spread? To these questions we now turn our attention.

Notes

1. Nkparom C. Ejituwu, "Warfare and Diplomacy in the Niger Delta," in Toyin Falola, *Warfare and Diplomacy in Pre-Colonial Nigeria* (Madison, 1992), pp. 199-207.
2. *Ibid.*
3. Mary Kingsley, *West African Studies* (London, 1899) quoted in Dike, *Trade and Politics in the Niger Delta* (Oxford, 1956), p. 19.
4. Ejituwu, *op. cit.* (Madison, 1992), pp 199-207.
5. This is what is called "Political Niger Delta." True Niger Delta comprises Delta, Ondo, Akwa Ibom, Rivers, Bayelsa and Cross River States.
6. Pereira, *op cit.* He called it "Jos."
7. S.I. Okoroafor, "Archaeological Investigation of the Niger Delta," (University of Port Harcourt, PhD Dissertation, 2007).
8. A.A. Derefaka. *Archaeology* and *Culture History in the Central Niger Delta* (Port Harcourt, Onyoma Research Publications, 2003).

9.   M.A.   Sowunmi,   "Late   Quartemery
      Environmental Change in Nigeria" in *Pollenet
      Spores*, Vol. XXII, No. 1,125-148.
10.   R. Horton, "Some Fresh Thoughts on Ijo
      Origins.   Expansion   and   Migrations"   in
      Nkparon C. Ejituwu, *op. cit* (1997).
11.   Okoroafor, *op cit*(2007), and F.J. Ellah, *Ali-
      Ogba: A History of the Ogba People* (Enugu,
      Fourth Dimension (1995).
12.   K.B. Erezene, "Living Together in the
      Niger Delta: A Historical Study of Itsekiri
      Relation in the 19th and 20th C." (Ph.D
      Seminar presented to the Department of
      History & Diplomatic Studies, University of
      Port Harcourt, 2008).
13.   M.D.W. Jeffreys, "Intelligence Report on
      the Andoni, 1930" and Ralph O.Ikuru, *Brief
      Manuscript History of Obolo (Andoni)* (1953).
14.   H. Nau, *We Move into Africa* (Missouri,
      1949).
15.   Westal B. Andah, *Some Nigerian Peoples
      (WAJA)* (Rex Charles Publication, 1993).

16. *Ibid.*
17. *Ibid.*
18. Horton, *op cit.,(\99&)*, pp. 226-227.
19. *Ibid*
20. *Ibid*
21. N. Nzewunwa, *A Source Book for Nigerian Archaeology* (Lagos, 1983).
22. Martha Anderson and P.M. Peek, *Ways of the Rivers* (Los Angeles, 2002).
23. Horton, *op cit* (1998).
24. Andah, *op cit* (1993). For the Ogoni on the Ghana issue, see Rev. (Dr.) S. Kpone-Tonwe of the University of Port Harcourt.
25. J.C. Anene, *Southern Nigeria in Transition* (London, 1966), p. 7.
26. Alagoa, *op cit.* (1972).
27. E.D.W. Opuogulaya personal communication (1991). Also, see Opuogulaya, in N.C. Ejituwu, *A History of Obolo (Andoni) in the Niger* Delta (1991), p. 253.
28. Tonye V. Erekosima, *Cultural Institutions* (1985). See also Pereira, *op cit.* (trans.) G.H.T.

Kimble, Esmeraldo de Situ Orbts (1937 p. 132.

29.   Asarama was probably Pereira's village in the creek with a population of 2,000 inhabitants. See Comte C.N. de Cardi, "Andoni River and Its Inhabitants" in Mary Kingsley, *West African Studies* (London, 1899), pp. 538-540.

30.   Horton, *op. cit.* (1998).

31.   E.D.W. Opu-Ogulaya, *op. cit.* (1991). See also, Opu-Ogulaya, *A Cultural Heritage of the Wakarike People* (Port Harcourt, 1975, p. 15). The law on fishing led to dispersal of some Obolo (Andoni) people. Among them were Kala-Ido in Kalabari, Okuru in Port Harcourt, Okoroete in Eastern Obolo, Ibeno in Akwa Ibom State, Egendem and Ataba in Andoni. See Nkparom C. Ejituwu, *A History of Obolo (Andoni) in the Niger Delta* (Oron, Manson and University of Port Harcourt Press, 1991).

32.   *Ibid.*

33.   The colonial administration had planned

it. See Jeffreys, "Intelligence Report on the Andoni (1930)."

34. Archbishop (Dr.) A. Adetiloye was caught in the "Andoni Flat." He was on his way to Ikuru Town (Andoni) in 1995 on Episcopal Mission. The idea is that he who enters it must quickly get out before he is grounded.

35. A.G. Leonard, *The Lower Niger and Its Tribes* (London, 1966), p.380. Leonard identified six priests in the Theocracy, with one of them (the *Obara-Yok*), being the High Priest of *Yok-Obolo*, p. 380.

36. A. Adonye *Fotnbo, A History of Bonny* (n.d.), pp. 129-131.

37. Tonye V. Erekosima, *Cultural Institutions* (1985).

38. J.H. Parry, *Europe and the Wider World* (Ibadan, 1964).

39. Chief Eric John Ikuru, Ngo, Andoni, 1975.

40. Elechi Amadi, *Ethics in Nigerian Culture* (London, 1984).

41. Hycient Iroanya Okere, "A History of

Indigenous Diplomatic Culture of Okehi"
(University of Port Harcourt, BA (Hons.)
History Project, 2008).

42.   Talbot, *op. cit.* (1926), p. 210.
43.   Alagoa, *The Small Brave City State* (Madison,
       1964).
44.   Barbot, *op. cit.* (Paris, 1732), pp. 462-463.
45.   Blessing Ngo, "The Alliance System in the
       Niger Delta, University of Port Harcourt BA
       Project (2008) pp. 1-6.

CHAPTER 3

Origins & Functions of the House of Skulls

3.1 Origins of the House of Skulls

A version of Obolo (Andoni) oral tradition says that the Obolo House of Skulls started with a quarrel of the Obolo with the Ohafia.[J] Details are not available but the Ohafia lived with the Obolo as *Mbem Owan*. But they refused to be integrated into the Obolo social system. This became a problem since it easily identified them as non-Obolo. Also, they specialized in head-hunting which made them economically identifiable Such problems arose when the Portuguese arrived Andoni in the 15th Century.[2]

The advent of the Portuguese soon caused a split between the Obolo and the Ohafia. The King of Andoni was willing to accept Christianity and sell his slaves to the Portuguese who wanted slaves and not fish or heads from head-hunting.[3]

But the Ohafia rejected Christianity and refused to stop head-hunting.[4]

Thereafter the Portuguese gave support to the Obolo and, ultimately, gave them guns and rums to encourage them to hunt down the Ohafia[5]. This was in about 1494[6].

When the Ohafia were not able to solve the problem, they decided to leave Andoni, but not before they had taught the Obolo people a lesson. That lesson was to engage them in a surprise attack and to behead as many Andoni men as they could.[7] That was not all. They also abducted as many women as they could and left Andoni, using the Imo River, for the hinterland Umuahia (Ibeku) and later, Ohafia[8].

Instead of burying the Obolo dead, *Yok-Obolo*, the national deity, decided that the "heads" be preserved as a memoriam of the conflict.[9] Then, the deity decreed that any Obolo killed by a stranger must be avenged. The head of such a stranger must be brought to the House of Skulls as a replacement of the head of the Obolo dead.[10] In this way, there developed a culture of "skulls keeping" in Obolo and the building of the House of Skulls as a memoriam of Obolo dead.

In 1699 Barbot saw in Dony Town, the capital of Andoni, and wrote:

> On the 24 July, 1699,1 went to the town of Dony ... Whose King is a very good-natured, civil man (who) speaks Portuguese and seems to have been instructed by the Romish Priests, who are sent over from time to time, from St. Tome and Brazil... I lay that night in the King's house, near his idol-house; and are kept there in a large press, full of the skulls of their enemies killed in war...[11]

The quotation above raises two questions; namely, the origins of the skulls - whether they were those of Obolo (Andoni) enemies or of Obolo heroes as claimed in the oral tradition? If they were those of Obolo (Andoni) heroes, the number of skulls would be small, consistent with African practice of "limited warfare". But, according to Barbot, the large press (House of Skulls) was "full of the skulls of (Andoni) enemies killed in war." So, the skulls were a combination of Obolo (Andoni) heads and of Obolo (Andoni) enemies, arising from the two hundred years of Obolo (Andoni) vengeance against Obolo (Andoni) enemies. It meant that the Obolo avenged the death of their heroes as directed by *Yok-Obolo*.

Of the origin of the House of Skulls, Barbot visited Bonny, Kalabari and other important towns of the Niger Delta that year but did not report the existence of such House of Skulls or such structures in these places. So the existence of the House of Skulls in Andoni is taken as the first in the Niger Delta[12].

Another possible origin of the House of Skulls was the environment of the Niger Delta. For instance, one cultural survival that may provide links on the origin of the cult is the prevalence up to the 19th century of the practice of head-hunting. For instance, the Ijo earned a reputation for war-likeness. Sometimes, a whole clan was united by a belief in a war-god, with war-heroes being entitled to wear the eagle feather as a mark of distinction.[13]

This practice, eventually led to the requirement that individuals interested in chieftaincy title must possess a skull or skulls as a qualification for the *peri* dance. Among the Etche, ritual head-hunting existed as early as the 16th century. And, it is possible that the need for the preservation of these skulls could be part of the origin of the concept of House of Skulls.[1] Also, reference must be made of African religious practices which invariably went with the requirement for human sacrifice. And what the people did with the skulls of victims of such sacrifices is a source of interest when asking about the origin of the House of Skulls.

3.2 Functions of the House of Skulls & General Analysis

Horton's periodization is interesting in many ways. First, it is interesting in its agreement with the dating of the presence of the Ohafia in Obolo

(Andoni). According to Horton, the age of head-hunting and fishing in the Eastern Niger Delta was about the 15th century[17] and it corresponded with the period when the Ohafia were head-hunting in Obolo (Andoni). By all indications, head-hunting occupied this period in the economic history of the Eastern Niger Delta.[18]

Further, because of the limited warfare practiced by Africans in these days, it is possible that the initial heads from the battle of the Ohafia and Obolo (Andoni) were few. And the dating of the battle was the late 15th century.[19] By 1699, when Barbot came to Dony Town, some two hundred years had elapsed and the Obolo (Andoni) may have added more heads, following their crusade for vengeance against the death of their brothers. The Obolo claimed that the battle with the Ohafia was their worst military encounter with any group in the Niger Delta [20].

Thus, what Barbot saw and described as "heads of Andoni enemies killed in war" may be correct after all; and it may be accepted as descriptive of the correct picture of what Barbot saw in Andoni. However, the original motive for Obolo (Andoni) keeping the skulls was not emphasized. Subsequent interpretation of Barbot and other European traders must certainly have wiped off the original motive and functions of the House of Skulls as no one thought or cared for the original concept of the Obolo for keeping the skulls. This is probably the greatest contribution of this work to Niger Delta scholarship on this issue.

It must not be forgotten that the Ohafia also abducted Obolo (Andoni) women whom they carried away from Obolo (Andoni).[23] There are many issues connected with this and we will try to look at some of them below:

Probably more relevant to the issue is that *Yok-Obolo* does not allow the Obolo (Andoni) to kill a woman or women in war, whether such a woman or women were Obolo (Andoni) or not.[24] This is sacrosanct as it serves as the foundation of Andoni warfare.[25] In other words, the "females" are very important in Obolo (Andoni) social system.

Sometimes the discussion of the issue of Obolo (Andoni) women extends to the issue of marriage of Obolo (Andoni) women by "strangers." Marriage of Andoni women by strangers was usually not allowed. According to Ralph O. Ikuru, Obolo (Andoni) women married "strangers" only in "diplomatic" situations, such as during a settlement of war when both sides had to exchange wives between the leaders of the warring groups.[26] In this way, Andoni women had the opportunity of producing nobles such as Kings, Princes and others nobles in their places of domicile. The Kings of Bonny or Opobo were Andoni by their mothers[27]. Wari, a seventeenth century King of Bonny, was Andoni by his mother.[28] So was Chief Cookey-Gam of Opobo Town who was Andoni by his mother as well.[29] According to Ralph O. Ikuru, also, many of these women performed creditably that there developed the tradition among Niger Delta nobles of regarding their marriages as incomplete until they had added an Obolo (Andoni) woman to their harems [30]. This claim would invariably make Andoni indispensable in the social development of the Niger Delta.

Another scenario is the observation that when an Obolo (Andoni) man was dissatisfied with his marriage, he, invariably, started off to Umuahia-Ibeku for wife. The latter was, probably, where the Ohafia dumped Andoni women whom they had abducted when they were leaving the Niger Delta for the hinterland. But, because of the limited warfare practiced by Africans at that time, the number of such women carried away from Andoni would have been few. As a whole, Igboland remained a source of wives for Niger Delta people in the 19th century and beyond.

In conclusion, not much is known about the Ohafia. However, they called themselves Mbem Owan and did a lot of head-hunting when they were in Andoni. They also rejected the Portuguese and Christianity which brought them into difficulty with the Andoni and the Portuguese.

That the Ohafia had lived in the Niger Delta is

a truism. Their tradition and that of Obolo (Andoni) confirm it. It is also evident in their lifestyle. It was they who served as the linch-pin in the Calabar-Fernando Poo smuggling trade of the 1950's which was a maritime affair.[31] Thus, they are riverine people despite the fact that they now live in Igbo heartland.

A great deal of cordial relationship exists between the Obolo and the Ohafia. Any major ceremony in Obolo (Andoni) must bring Ohafia people to Andoni for participation. Okwala, the deserted Ohafia village, is still there, and can be visited any time. People are, however, advised not to be aggressive with persons seen on its road or in the village as such persons could be ghosts.

The Obolo call the Ohafia their "brothers" and easily inter-marry with them.[32] And, there is evidence that Ohafia leaders easily welcome Obolo people to Ohafia. In fact, a student who visited Ohafia had written that Ohafia people are Obolo (Andoni) in diaspora. That is how far the relationship has gone[33].

Notes

1. Chief Dixon C. Otoko (c. 80) at a public interview in Agwut Obolo (1974).
2. *Ibid*
3. *ibid* The Ohafia lived in Andoni with the name: "Mbem Owan" and claimed to have come from Benin territory. According to Arua, the Ohafia may have forgotten their early history but not the fact that they had lived with the Andoni in the Eastern Niger Delta. See A.O. Arua, *A Short History of Ohafia* (Enugu, 1951). Also, see fn, 6 below.
4. *Ibid*. Also, Tonye V. Erekosima, *Cultural Institutions* (Port Harcourt, 1985).
5. *Ibid*.
6. Paul Ndukwe (c. 50) of Amaekpor, Ohafia, interviewed in Port Harcourt 27th August, 1985, Also, Ndukwe, "Settlement Pattern and Social Structure of the Ohafia" (University of Port Harcourt B.Sc (Sociology) Thesis, 1985). The Obolo (Andoni) today regard the Ohafia

as one of their people in diaspora and point to their settlement of Okwala on Andoni Mainland that is still a deserted village. The Ohafia occasionally come to Andoni as homecoming particularly on ceremonial occasions such as in 1993 when they came for the *Nkwak* (victory war dance) at Agwut Obolo.

7. *Ibid*
8. *Ibid.*
9. Chief Dixon C. Otoko, *op. cit.* {1974). Among the Oron, who are said to relate to the Obolo (Andoni), when an illustrious Oron man died, his image was carved in iron wood and kept in an *Ekpu* as a memoriam. See Philip O, Nsugbe "Oron Ekpu Figures," *Nigeria Magazine*, Vol. 71 (1961), pp. 357-359. The relationship between *Ekpu and* the "House of Skulls" is yet to be studied.
10. Ejituwu, "Yok-Obolo: The Influence of a Traditional Religion on the socio-cultural life of the Andoni," *Africa: Journal of the Institute of*

African Studies, Vol. 65,1 (Cambridge, 1995), pp. 97-113. A.G. Leonard, *The Lower Niger and Its Tribes* (London, 1906), p.380

11. Barbot, *Description of the Coast of North and South Guinea* (Paris, 1732), pp. 462-463. The lapse of time between 1699, when Barbot visited Andoni, and 1494 when the Ohafia left Andoni, is about 200 years. Also, E. J. Alagoa, *op. cit.* (Ibadan, 1972), p.154.

12. Alagoa, *op. cit.* (Ibadan, 1972), p. 154.

13. *Ibid.*

14. Hycient Iroanya Okere, "A History of Indigenous Diplomatic Culture of Okehi" (University of Port Harcourt B.A. Hons, Project, 2008).

15. *Ibid.* Also, Philip O. Nsugbe, "Oron Ekpu Figures," in *Nigeria Magazine* (1961), 71, pp. 357-59.

16. Ndukwe, *op. cit.* (1985).

17. Professor Robin Horton in a personal communication (1999).

18. *Ibid.*

19. Ndukwe,*op cit.* (1985).
20. *Ibid.*
21. This is probably the serious beginning of head-hunting among the Obolo (Andoni) as dictated by the national deity, *Yok-Obolo.* See fn. 32.
22. Barbot, *op. cit.* (1732)., pp. 462-464.
23. Chief Dixon, *op cit.* (1974).
24. Ndukwe, *op. cit.* (1985).
25. M.D.W. Jeffreys, "Intelligence Report on the Andoni (1930)". (NA/E CP. 7237 Minloc. 6/1/135).
26. *Ibid.*
27. Ralph O. Ikuru, *Manuscript Brief History of Obolo (Andoni)* (Ikuru Town. 1953). Andoni women had complained that Andoni backwardness was a function of the marriage system that kept the women away from men of other ethnic groups. See also Nkparom C. Ejituwu and A,I. Gabriel, *Women in Nigerian History: Rivers and Bayelsa States Experience* (Port Harcourt,1999).
28. Ralph O. Ikuru, *op. cit.* (1953).
29. Also, *op. cit.* (1972).

30. Ralph O. Ikuru, *op. cit.* (1953). According to Chief Dixon C. Otoko, marriage between Bonny, Opobo and Andoni had produced so much in personnel that for Andoni to go to war with Bonny or Opobo would be an exercise in futility as it would only lead to the shedding of Obolo (Andoni) blood, See Dixon C. Otoko of Agwut Obolo, in a personal communication (1974).

31. *Ibid.*

32. *Ibid.* Also, Jennifer E. Kalu. According to her Andoni women were not "dumped" in Umuahia-Ibeku but were shared and married off by Ibeku men while the remaining ones were carried off to Ohafia by Mbem men who were afraid that Andoni and their Portuguese friends were on their trail. Jennifer E. Kalu (University of Port Harcourt BA Long Essay, 2008). Some Andoni say that Rev. (Dr.) Umar Ukpai sometimes visited Andoni as home coming.

33. Peter Ereforokuma, "Obolo (Andoni) in Diaspora" (University of Port Harcourt BA Long Essay, 1992).

CHAPTER 4

The Spread of the House of Skulls

4.1 Introduction

The idea that the spread of the concept of the House of Skulls was a function of its value to the city-states is a truism. But that it originated from Dony Town because European traders saw it there in 1699 and nowhere else has to be speculative. For instance, the House of Skulls in Ogoni territory was not reported, yet we know that they had one, located in Sii, in Khana Local Government Area, which is immediately north of Andoni.[1] Accordingly, there may be Houses of Skulls which were not recorded by European traders but were there in the Niger Delta and Delta hinterland.

4.2 The Niger Delta

As we saw earlier, the House of Skulls was seen in Andoni in 1699, the late 17th century. By the 19th century, its existence in Bonny, Kalabari and other parts of the Delta had been reported. Rev. Hope Waddell, visiting Bonny in the 1850's, saw the House of Skulls as part of the paraphernalia of *Ikuba,* the national god of Bonny.[2] He described it as "a horrid place half-filled with human skulls and other unsightly objects, a pyramid of them reaching from the ground to the roof.[3]

Alagoa gave insight into the development of the House of Skulls in Bonny. He said, for instance,

> Queen Kambasa (of Bonny) is said to have built a house of skulls as part of the cult following a successful war against the Ogoni. But this house of Skulls and the use of the monitor lizard *(Varanus niloticus)* the sacred animal of *Ikuba* did not gain maturity before the 18th century... This interpretation of a late flowering of this cult is suggested because, in 1699 James Barbot reported Iguana worship, complete with a house of skulls full of the skulls of enemies killed in war among the Andoni (Dony) but not at

Bonny... In the 19th century Barbot's description became applicable to Bonny where the Christians complained of the "house of Skulls.

Also, Sir Harry Johnson, Vice-Consul for the Bight of Biafra, described the *Iguana* cult in Bonny as being very strong for it was dangerous to kill the animal there.[6] This was the level of esteem attached to the monitor lizard as an integral part of the culture of Bonny and, before long, the King of Bonny had had the European traders produce, in bronze, a cast of the monitor lizard for him.

The House of Skulls and the cult of the Iguana probably spread from Andoni to Bonny through Wari, a late 17th century King of Bonny with an Andoni mother.[5] He is said to be a lover of culture, particularly music and dancing and wanted Bonny to benefit from his Andoni background.[6]

The House of Skulls was also seen in Kalabari in the 19th century. There, the skulls were placed on *Ebeka*, a rack full of the skulls of their enemies killed in war[7]. Ironically, the national goddess, *Owamekaso*, abhorred the shedding of blood in Kalabari territory. Thus, some Kalabari male gods, *Okpolodo* and *Siri-Opubo*, whose existence, in fact, pre-dated the arrival of *Owamekaso*, had their rituals cannibalistic. Men interested in the *peri* title, which required the display of heads as symbols of bravery, went afield for such trophies of war. Also, strangers in Kalabari who refused or were unable to integrate culturally, stood the risk of being killed. Slaves or strangers among the Kalabari who did not learn to speak the Kalabari language quickly and, therefore, could not respond to certain pass-words uttered in the night by cult members, were seized and killed.[8] It is possible that heads obtained from this source formed part of the *Ebeka*.

The contradiction apparent in the injunction of *Owamekaso* against shedding of blood in Kalabari territory and the predilection of *Siri-Opubo* for blood shedding, was resolved by Kalabari people doing most of their warlike activities at *Namasibi*, a veritable golgotta, located far from the abode of the goddess. The warriors returned home, looking clean and innocent. Also, they performed certain purification rites acceptable to the goddess. But, by all means, the concept of House of Skulls, as an integral part of warfare and diplomacy, was practiced by Kalabari people.[9]

In Nembe and Okrika, it was the same. *Ogidiga,* the national deity of Nembe, required the sacrifice of captives of war and the preservation of their skulls in *Egbesu* (House of Skulls).[10] This is clear in the account of the Akassa Raids of 1895 in which, Brass traders assaulted the Royal Niger Company Factories at Akassa, taking many men and women to Nembe where some of them were sacrificed to *Ogidiga* and their skulls preserved in the *Egbesu.*[11]

In Okrika, *Fenibeso,* the national deity, was extremely warlike. Okrika people sacrificed their war victims at *Ilachingi,* Ihe Shrine of the deity in Okrika town. There also, particularly during *Toru Ohua* ceremony, honours were conferred on those fighters who had returned from battle with heads or had fought gallantly. So influential had the cult of

Fenibeso been that his cells could be found, not only among Okrika settlements, but also among the Kalabari settlements of Soku, Ikulema, Kula, Agbalama and Miniama[12].

Even the newly found Opobo Town had a similar story to tell. Opobo Town rose in Andoni from the dusts of 1869 Bonny civil war. No sooner had Jaja established as King of the new settlement than he started to demonstrate his understanding of Niger Delta trade and politics. In 1881, for instance, he sent about fifty war-canoes to Ikot Utip, one of the Ibeno villages whose inhabitants had refused to trade with him. The punitive raid is said to have brought back to Opobo Town some Ibeno men, women and children, some of who were forced into acknowledging King Jaja as King of Ibeno while others were killed to obtain skulls in the spirit of fee time. Of this, Talbot writes:

> At day-light on 10 April 1881, fifty canoes belonging to Jaja and flying

British flag' - arrived (Ibeno) with breech-loading cannon and riffles, and bombarded the villages of Ikoretu, Ikoutah, Ebotiyan, Obarechan and Empanek, plundered and burnt them and took one hundred prisoners because the people refused to trade with him but instead helped Watts - the prisoners, chiefly women and children, were slaughtered at Opobo, some of Jaja's own children cutting off the heads of the - Kwa Ibo children in order that they might earn the right to wear the eagle's plume - a distinction which was only granted to those who had killed a man....[13]

In this statement, we see a Delta people in real action, action explainable in terms of the value of skulls and houses of skulls as dynamics of trade and politics in the area.

Whether or not Opobo Town had a House of Skulls, is not certain. But, in terms of the acquisition of skulls in the spirit and traditions of the time, King Jaja allowed his men to kill to qualify to wear "eagle's plumes." So, it is evident that the tradition of keeping skulls as a symbol of national power had, by the 19th century, become general to the Eastern Delta States, where it further influenced other aspects of their culture.

4.3 The Hinterland

Much as the cult of House of Skulls was spreading in the Delta, so did it spread to the hinterland. Here again, emphasis is on lack of documentation of the cult in this region. Europeans did not get here until the 19th century. And it was then we begin to read of the existence of the House of Skulls. But the tradition may have been there before the arrival of European traders as evident in *Things Fall Apart* (London, Heinemann Educational Books, 1958) by Chinua Achebe, where Okonkwo, for instance, led the people of Umuofia to war and returned with heads as symbols of victory in the war.[14] Also, when the gods demanded the head of Ikemefuna as a means of returning the people to the land, he was sacrificed. Whether the skulls were preserved and how they were preserved, we do not know.

However, this study may start with the question of the migration of Ohafia from the Niger Delta. Oral evidence from both Ohafia and Andoni say that the Ohafia migrated from Andoni. A version of the tradition of migration from Andoni speaks of Ohafia's House of Skulls[15] and the question is whether they had the practice of keeping skulls like the Andoni and, by implication, became the source of the spread of this practice to the hinterland.

The Ohafia dated their migration from the Eastern Delta to about the 15th century,[16] an antiquity which suggests that they might have been the carriers of the culture from the Delta to the hinterland. Besides, their south-north movement was unique in that it was probably, the only known major movement of people from the Eastern Delta into the hinterland.

There is no argument that an Ohafia man

must, in those ancient days, present skulls to
kamalu, their national deity. Also, oral evidence
indicates that, for a youth to be initiated into
manhood and allowed to marry, he must possess
a skull as a symbol of his maturity and bravery.
However, there is no indication of the existence
of a house of skulls among the Ohafia. Rather, a
man kept the skull or skulls that he had earned
from a war or wars. And when he had
successfully got three skulls, he became a special
member of the society, able to "drink palm-wine
from a ritual pot."[17]

Also, the Ohafia displayed a war-dance in
which the head-gear originally contained some
human skulls. Today, such dance is only
ceremonial, often carried out to entertain visitors
on important occasions. Such social different-
tiation carried different degrees of status
symbols. The one that had marked effect on the
male adult population was the distinction
between the *Ufiein* (war heroes) in battle and the
Ujo (cowards). The former was entitled to wear

an eagle's plum and the red tail-feather of a parrot as a token of bravery in battle. At death, an *Ufiein* was honoured with *Okerekwa* (dance for a dead war hero). On the other hand, the *Ujo* was a status of shame and degradation. An *Ujo's* life was marked by humiliation of civic disabilities which made death preferable. He might even be denied the privilege of marriage. And, if he married, his wife was denied many social privileges such as not being allowed to wear "George cloth," bracelets, armlets of brass or elephant tusks which were suitable in those days.

The Ohafia were probably the most warlike group among the Igbo. But they fought wars for glory which made their warfare appear indiscriminate and the people easily exploitable by their neighbours, like the Aro, who were not a race of warriors but fought wars for political and economic ends.[18]

Similarly, the Ndoki, Oguta and Aro were very much associated with the cult of House of Skulls; and their examples demonstrate the various uses made of human skulls in the Niger Delta and hinterland societies. For instance, among the Ndoki, human skulls were used by their owners as "foot stools," as symbols of their victory over their enemies and as warning to future generations that the possessors were men of war.[19] Also, no man became a chief in Oguta unless he had acquired a skull. Gradually, the importance attached to the acquisition of skulls led to the rise, among them, of the *Igbu* Society (Killer Society).[20]

When acquisition of human skulls became progressively difficult, Oguta people shifted from head-hunting to the killing of leopards because, the latter represents the test of manhood as leopards were very strong and dangerous. And, in some communities, the wearing of leopard skin was regarded as a symbol of leadership.[21]

When leopards died off or migrated into the depth of the forests and it became almost impossible to get them, Oguta people shifted from killing of leopards or human beings to the purchase of human skulls from those who possessed them. In this way, they bastardized the original concept of skulls as a symbol of strength and prowess. But, it was still significant in that, at least, some measures of ability was evident, for such skulls were, invariably, expensive and possession meant wealth and affluence, which is another index of strength and intelligence within the context of the culture of that time[22].

Where the concept of House of Skulls was fully accomplished in the hinterland was among the Aro. Colonial officers in Igboland were very clear about the size of the Aro House of Skulls and how it was built up. They described it as "a legendary pyramid of human skulls;" and the Aro as controlling the Igbo and Ibibio. [23] As said earlier, the Aro were not a race of warriors, but, by using the Ohafia and others, they were able to build a large house of skulls. According to Uka,

When the Aro, in their travels, realized that the people of Ohafia Division had a consuming passion for head-hunting, they formed alliances with village groups of Ohafia and Abam... Under the contract, the Aro were to seek out territories to be attacked and report to Ohafia and Abam people, who themselves were only out for heads. Any town, therefore, having a dispute with another and wishing to wreck summary vengeance on it, would apply through the Aro agents for a force of Ohafia and Abam warriors.[24]

And, by this means, they exercised considerable influence and dominance over a large area from the Niger Delta to the Cross River Basin which were then the centres of the overseas trade.

The secret of the Aro supremacy was their deity, *Ibiniukpabi* (Long Juju). By various diplomatic means, the Aro popularized the oracle and men came from far and wide, including the Niger Delta, to consult him. So successful was the cult that all an Aro man had to do was to identify himself and he was able to move, unscathed, from one end of the Eastern Region to the other in those days of the slave trade when such journeys were extremely unsafe. Also, so powerful was the oracle that *Kamalu-* (Thunder), the High Priest of *Ibiniukpabi*, took "a new wife every market day" (a statement that could only be understood symbolically since a new market day came every four or eight days and one cannot understand how a man can accumulate such number of wives arising from the practice).[25] But the import of the name, "Thunder" as well as his ability to marry any girl of his choice, is clear; it is an indication of the power of the deity. The most reliable evidence of the deity as powerful was the House of Skulls which was pyramidal.

So, both the Niger Delta and the hinterland shared common ideas and customs about the House of Skulls. Also, with minor exceptions, the symbolisms of the House of Skulls among the Niger Delta and the hinterland people were the same; which is probably what Isichei meant when she writes that "Igbo fought wars for glory."[26] The similarity in meaning and symbolisms was a product

of the proximity of the two areas and the inter-
dependence of one on the other for economic
survival.

4.4 Symbolism of the House of Skulls
All said and done, the spread of the House of Skulls
was a function of the political and economic value of
the institution. Also, as a symbol of the military
disposition of its owners, it was an image of power.
And power was absolutely necessary in the Delta
environment in contact with European traders who
encouraged warfare as a factor in the acquisition of
slaves and palm oil. Power, wealth and warfare
became inseparable; and they meant weapons such as
cannons, cannon-balls and other fire-arms brought by
European traders to the Niger Delta; and any group
that neglected them became a victim of inter-group
conflict and monopolistic capitalism.

The quest for skulls increased warfare and this
further led to the acquisition of more wealth,
influence and power. To demonstrate their wealth
and power, delta people built their individual

houses of skulls. And to preserve and maintain the structure, they accumulated more arms and ammunition, purchased more slaves to serve as *pullaboys and* soldiers. These men manned the canoes, trade routes and markets of each of the city-states. It soon led to the rise of the "House System" in Bonny, Kalabari, Okrika, Opobo, Nembe and other Niger Delta city-states.[27] The nucleus of the "House System" was the "war canoe" house, a warlike institution designed to enable each city-state effectively prosecute the overseas trade. By this system, each city-state was broken into "houses," a "house" being a unit of social organization and relation of production. An essential factor in the 'war-canoe' house system was that its social components were made up, not of kins and blood relations, but of individuals, some of who might have been of slave origins; and each "war-canoe" house was to develop and maintain a "war-canoe," which served as a unit of the city-state. It was this factor that emphasized, not lineage and blood relations, but ability and demonstration of valour, economic and martial skills. Ultimately, slaves who demonstrated these qualities had the hope of being elevated to positions of greatness, King Jaja being an example of a slave who became a king. The aggregate of the "Houses" constitutes the city-state over which was the King, the supreme political leader of the metropolis.[28]

The factor that made the war-canoe house possible was the availability of arms and ammunition. The overseas trade made it possible for inhabitants of the Delta city-states to have access to arms and ammunition in large quantities. Since the 16th century, ammunition available in Europe include arms such as Sneiders, Matinis and Percussion guns. From about the 16th century, European traders were willing to sell these weapons to Delta people as a means of attaining their own economic ends.[29] In this way, the European traders encouraged the "Devil's Theory" of war to play out.

Finally, apart from weapons and arms, there was the direct intervention and involvement of the

European traders in some of the campaigns. The weapons were meaningless without the economic order that stimulated their supply and use. Delta people, originally, supplied fish and other products of their environment; but European traders wanted slaves and later, when slave trade was abolished, palm oil. The role of the European traders and the development of the House of Skulls are important. They did not only supply the arms; sometimes, they actually got involved in inter-communal conflicts. There were many instances of this in the Niger Delta, and in the Cross River region. In the Cross River region, Isaac Parker, a European trader in Calabar in 1765, accompanied an Efik Chief on many slave-catching expeditions. He writes:

The canoes were fitted out with ammunition, cutlasses, pistols, cannon balls and had two, three pounder cannons, one fixed in the bows, and the other in the stem. On the first expedition, they paddled up the river

until they came to a village, hid in the bush
until night; then seized everyone they
could see. At another village, they took 45
slaves. About a forthnight later, they made a
similar expedition.[30]

In the Niger Delta, it was the same. As we noted
earlier, in 1704, John Grazilhier hunted elephants
with the King of Andoni.[31] One may argue that this
is not a good example. But, involving the use of
weapons such as "muskets, cutlasses, lances, saws,
etc.;" it has implications for inter-communal
conflicts. When European traders were not directly
involved, they gave support to local people in their
wars with neighbours and when trouble arose,
they intervened. In the Andoni-Bonny war of
1846, Andoni defeated Bonny and killed their two
leaders; and then closed the trade route to the
hinterland markets[32]. When the war was
documented, it was Andoni that was documented
as the defeated. This is probably what Alagoa
meant when he said that the war of 1846 was

ended through the good offices of the British traders at Bonny in 1846.[33]

Also, in the invasion of Ibeno in 1881, it was they who encouraged King Jaja to fly the British flag as an indication of the British Government support of the latter in his campaign for control of the trade of the Qua Iboe area. Consul Hewett made it clear to the Foreign Office, London, that King Jaja was encouraged by European traders in Opobo who were interested in furthering their businesses.[34] Baikie complained to the Foreign Office, London, in 1857 that "No person can visit the (Niger Delta) without hearing of deeds performed by European Captains and supercargoes which, although attested, are almost incredible." He said further, I have heard admitted by perpetrators or been told by sufferers and by eye witnesses deeds and actions, the revelation of which I hesitate to commit to paper. One of these deeds was the Andoni-Bonny Treaty of 1846 which he described as "a Diplomatic Curiosity."[35]

All these have implications for conflicts to arise and the erection of Houses of Skulls.

Notes

1. Chief G.U. Ewaye in a personal communication (1974).
2. Report of the Proceedings of the Second Session of the Fourth Synod of the Diocese of the Niger Delta held at St. Michael's Church, Aba, 30th April - 3rd May, 1992, p. 18; Hope Waddell, *Journal*, 26 December, 1849. Also, D.C. Crowther, *The Niger Delia Church Pastorate* (London, 1907), p.27.
3. *Ibid.*
4. E.J. Alagoa and A. Fombo, A *Chronicle of Grand Bonny* (Ibadan, 1972).
5. William Baikie, *Narrative of an Exploring Voyage* (London, 1856).
6. Alagoa, *op. cit.* (Ibadan, 1972), p. 154.
7. Robin Horton of the University of Port

Harcourt, 2nd April, 1990.

8. *Ibid.*

9. Horton, "Kalabari World-View," in *Africa* (London, 1962).

10. Alagoa, *The Small Brave City State* (Wisconson, 1964).

11. *Ibid*

12. Chief A.S. Abam in a personal communication, Port Harcourt, 2nd October 1992. Also, E.D.W. Opu-Ogulaya, *A Cultural Heritage of the Wakirike People* (Port Harcourt, 1975), p. 15.

13. P.A. Talbot, *Peoples of Southern Nigeria*, Vol. I (London, 1926), p. 210. Also, killing of the Ibeno, who are Adonni, was a violation of the Obolo-Opobo Treaty of 1869; hence, King Jaja claimed that he took 'peravission' from Adonni leaders on the western side of the Imo River to 'chastise' them, see Ejituwu, op. cit (1991), pp. 146-147.

14. Chinua Achebe, *Things Fall Apart* (London, Heinemann Educational Books, 1958).

15. Chief Paul Ndukwe (Port Harcourt, 1985). Also,

see Peter Ereforokuma, "Andoni in Diaspora" (University of Port Harcourt BA (Hons.) History Thesis, 1992). Hope Waddell, *op cit* Africans may be barbaric, but Europeans were not less so.

16. Elizabeth Isichei. *Igbo Worlds* (London, 1977), p. 210.

17. Ikenna Nzimiro, *Studies in Ibo Political System* (Berkeley, Los Angeles, 1972), pp. 2-36), Also, Elizabeth Isichei, *Igbo Worlds* (London, 1977), K-.O. Dike, Felicia Ekejiuba, *The Aro of South-Eastern Nigeria, 1650- 1950* (London, 1990). And A.E. Afigbo, *The Igbo and Their* Neighbours (Ibadan, 1987), pp. 45-47. Also, Jan Vansina of the University of Wisconsin in a personal interview, (1986).

18. *Ibid.*

19. E.A. Onwuzirike, "Mbaise Under Colonial Rule" (University of Port Harcourt PhD Dissertation, 1992). Also J.U.J. Asiegbu, *Nigeria and Its British Invaders (New* York, 1984). Also, K.O. Dike and Felicia Ekejuiba, *The Aro of South Eastern Nigeria* (Ibadan, 1990). Also, Elizabeth Isichei, *Igbo*

Worlds (London, 1977).
20. Nzimiro, *op. cit.* (Los Angeles, 1972), pp. 2-36.
21. Isichei, *Igbo Worlds* (London, 1977).
22. *Ibid.* Also, Nzimiro, op. cit. (1972).
23. *Ibid* According to Prof. P.D. Curtin of the University of Wisconsin, Madison, Wisconsin. (1972), there were two types of cannibalism in pre-colonial Africa, namely, ritual and gustatory cannibalism. It was mostly ritual cannibalism that Africans practiced. *Osu* system of the Igbo was a form of ritual cannibalism in which human flesh was not tasted. Also, see P.D. Curtin, *The Image of Africa (Madison, 1964).*
24. *N. Uka,* "A Note on Abam Warriors of Igboland" *Warfare and Diplomacy in Igboland* (1972).
25. Elspeth Huxley, *Four Guineas* (London, Reprint Society, 1954), p,283 quoted in Epelle, *op cit* (Aba, 1972), p. 2. For details, see Alan Burns *History of Nigeria* (London, 1978), p. 147.

26. Elizabeth Isichei, *Igbo Worlds* (1977).

27. Alagoa, "The Development of Institutions in the Niger Delta," *op cit.*

28. *Ibid.* Alagoa, *op cit.* (Ibadan), 1972), p. 154. Also, Nkparom C. Ejituwu, "The Andoni-Bonny Treaty of 1846: A Diplomatic Curiosity" in *ODU: Journal of West African Studies,* Vol. 36, (July, 1989), pp. 57-74. Also, Ejituwu, "The Political Economy of the Andoni-Bonny Treaty of 1846" in Yakubu A. Ochefu (ed.) *Oral Tradition, Totems and Nigerian Cultural History* (Makurdi, 2008), pp. 55-66.

29. *Ibid.*

30. Monday Abasiattai. *A History of Cross Rivers Region of Nigeria* (Enugu, 1990).

31. Barbot, *op. cit* (1732), pp. 462-463.

32. H. Webber, "Intelligence Report on Bonny Tribe (1931)" (NA/ICSO 26 27226); p. 28.

33. Alagoa, *op. cit.* (1972), p. 154. See Dike, *Trade and Politics in the Niger Delta* (Oxford, 1956).

34. Baikie, *op. cit.* (London, 1856).

35. *Ibid.*

CHAPTER 5

The Collapse of the House of Skulls

5.1 Introduction

The collapse of the House of Skulls was a function of the turmoil that followed the trade of the Niger Delta. By 1807 the slave trade had officially stopped in favour of palm oil trade. While the slave trade existed, the issue of morality was not emphasized and both African and European traders jointly engaged in it. But with the end of the slave trade and the rise of the palm oil trade, Europeans began to claim superiority consequent on the evolution of the concept of Social Darwinism with its inner core concept of the survival of the fittest. Africans were no longer seen as equal to the Europeans. It was racism all the way and many African institutions were affected.[1]

5.2 The Collapse of the House of Skulls

The House of Skulls was destined to collapse. By

1906, there was hardly any of it left in the Niger Delta and the hinterland. The collapse was a function of the internal and external changes that occurred in the Delta environment. Before the 19th century, Delta middlemen were successful in holding their own and keeping European traders at the coast. Some of the European traders were, in character, quite crude and predisposed to flout the regulations and laws of the area. The House of Skulls and other warlike institutions of their hosts and trade partners, served as warnings to such European traders. From Barbot, it appeared that European traders were "respectful" of the Andoni cult. He said that "Anyone of them who touched the cult objects without permissions was likely to be severely punished and in danger of losing his life."[2]

Similarly, Elspeth Huxley, writing of the experience in Bonny, says: "when two Liverpool seamen, rolling a cask of water, accidentally killed a monitor lizard, the king sentenced them to death."[3] Thus, there is no doubt that Delta middlemen were generally able to maintain undisputed control of the affairs of their locality, But from the 1830's when the Lander Brothers, Richard and John Lander, discovered that the Niger River empties its waters into the Atlantic ocean, the interest of European traders shifted from the earlier arrangement by which they remained at the coast while African middlemen and partners linked them with the hinterland. It was one expedition after another until 1854 when Dr. Baikie successfully demonstrated the safety of Europeans by using quinine as prophylactic against malaria. Europeans intensified their search for hinterland markets and subsequently demonstrated their superiority in military technology.

First, there was a breakdown of former non-violent relations. This was followed by the intervention of the British government and the establishment of British institutions in the Niger Delta. The first was the appointment of a British Consul for the Bight of Biafra in 1849, followed by the establishment of the Court of Equity in Bonny in 1854 which, in the same year, exiled the King. But, first, let us see how the local people contributed to the fall of the House of Skulls.[4]

By the 19th century, European presence had started to influence the attitude of the local people. Diplomacy was then characterized by "lies" and "trickery," all in the attempt to monopolise the advantages of contact with European traders. In Bonny and Kalabari, "lying" (Bonny) and "cunning" (Kalabari) became the strongest tools of success with the European traders. Bonny had possibly borrowed the concept of the House of Skulls from the Obolo (Andoni) and built the largest House of Skulls in the Niger Delta. But that was not all; she also produced a document to show that she conquered Obolo (Andoni), probably the most powerful military force in the Eastern Niger Delta in the 19th century (Baikie, 413).

In Kalabari, King Amakiri IV had indicated that he needed the Christian Mission to Christianize his people. But, in actual fact, he brought them only to help his children learn how to sell the palm oil better. Unable to withstand this cunning, the missionaries left for Okrika where they established St. Peter's Anglican Church successfully. In Opobo Town, it was the same. When questioned about his action against the Ibeno, King Jaja claimed that his invasion of Ibeno was to enable him "chastise his subjects."[6] Yet, King Jaja had no evidence to support his claim that the Ibeno were his subjects. The Ibeno had merely opposed his commercial interest and favoured direct contact with the European traders.[7]

However, nowhere was the fraudulent spirit of the time better demonstrated than in the method used by the Aro to acquire human skulls for the Shrine of *Ibiniukpabi*. As said earlier, the Aro were not a warlike people and so they had to use other warlike people to acquire slaves and skulls for their purpose. Also, they exploited the reverence people had for the oracle, *Ibiniukpabi*. Of this, Baikie said,

When a man goes to Aro to consult Tshuku, he is received by some of the priests outside of the town near a small stream. Here, he makes an offering after which a fowl was killed and if it appears unpropitiable a quantity of red dye, probably camwood, is spilt into the water, which the priests tell the people is blood, and on this the votary is hurried off by priests and is seen no more, it being given out that Tshuku has been displeased, and has taken him.[8]

The reality was that the "cunning" Aro sold such men to Efik and Delta middlemen who resold them to European traders. The "mountain of skulls" also suggests that some of them were sacrificed to *Ibiniukpabi*.

Fraud and other negative tendencies from both African and European sources led to social and economic instability which further led to the appointment of a British Consul for the Bights of Benin and Biafra to protect the lives and interests of British traders in the Delta. The appointment of the

Consul represented the formal intervention of the British Government in the affairs of the Delta people.

As said earlier, the Consul set up a Court of Equity in Bonny in 1854 and elsewhere for the settlement of disputes between African middlemen and European traders. Significantly, the chairman and members of the Court were largely Europeans which meant a decline in the capacity of Africans to control the affairs of their locality. Also, the administration of justice went largely European. For instance, whereas oath-taking and "swearing of the gods" had been the elements of justice fully understood by the people before, Bible, gun and the other symbols of western justice, introduced by the Court of Equity, were hardly meaningful. Thus, African traders went the way of the European "palm oil ruffians" who falsified documents and cheated rivals to make the best of the situation.

One good example of this was the Treaty of 1846, which was deliberately made to subvert the reality of the historical relations between Andoni

and Bonny in 1846. When in 1869, Jaja took oath of
submission with the Andoni, this evidence became
clear. But no sooner was King Jaja safe among the
Andoni people than he claimed ownership of the
Treaty document of 1846. Neither Jaja nor the
Ibeno, were signatory to the Treaty. But Jaja used it
as the basis of his invasion of Ibeno land in 1881.

After a quarrel with the British Consul, Edward
Hewett, over the document, the latter rushed to
Britain, produced a draft of the Protection
Treaties,[9] which, in content and structure, were
not different from the "Bonny document." Hewett
returned to the Delta in May, 1884 not only with
the already prepared document but also with
presents of drinks, cloths and bright beads (as
bribes) to encourage easy signing of the Protection
Treaties. One of the first victims of the new move
was no less than King Jaja who was made to sign
the document and, on signing it, was exiled from
Opobo and the Niger Delta. Thereafter, the Ibeno
were declared subjects of the Queen of England.
In fact, they were the first people in the Niger

Delta to be so declared.

Second, the period coincided with the rise of the evangelical movement in Britain. In the 1850s, the Niger Delta started to vibrate from that source. Reverend Hope Waddell of the Presbyterian movement visited Bonny in an attempt to Christianize the inhabitants of the city-state. Although his enterprise in the Niger Delta was largely unsuccessful, he called attention of the world to Bonny, with a House of Skulls as high as a "pyramid;" and Bonny, Andoni and Kalabari, the most "barbaric" of the people of the Niger Delta.[10] In this way, he indirectly initiated a process that led to the destruction of Bonny House of Skulls.

In 1898, a Christian, Chief Wariso Manilla Pepple, of Bonny destroyed the House of Skulls and gave the brass cast of the Iguana in the House of Skulls to the Missionaries." As Comte C.N. de Cardi puts it, "The Juju House of Bonny, once the greatest show-piece of the town, has now (1899) completely disappeared and its hideous content (skulls) scattered.[12]

From Bonny, Christianity spread to other Delta city-states. It spreads to Brass (1868), Kalabari (1875), Okrika (1885), Opobo (1887) and Andoni (1904). As in Bonny, the spread of Christianity meant doom for the traditional belief systems in these places for, as said earlier, it caused disunity in some of the city-states, making some of their social elements highly destructive of cult objects. Like Bonny, the political leaders of some of these states were exiled, King Jaja of Opobo was exiled. So was Chief Animiebere Otoko of Andoni and King Ibanichuka of Okrika, all of who were shabbily treated.

As said before, from about 1830 when the Lander Brothers discovered that the Niger River emptied its waters into the Atlantic Ocean, European traders who had been content to remain on the coast, had their eyes in the hinterland for greater profits. The reference to "civilization" is, on the one hand, a reference to the rise of the concept of racial superiority derived from Social Darwinism and, on the other hand, a reference to the technological superiority arising from the Industrial Revolution. Social Darwinism came in force in the 1850s, and institutionalized the concept of African inferiority; and superior European technology symbolized by the British "Gunboat" which ushered in the New Imperialism, and changed the British attitudes to the Niger Delta.

Before the 19th century, with Africans and European traders commonly involved in the slave trade, not many people questioned the racial position of Africans. Africans and Europeans dined together and the former had the opportunity of sending some of their children to Europe where they lived at the courts of Kings and Queens and were brought up as equal of the whiteman.[14] But with the end of the slave trade early in the 19th century and the rise of Social Darwinism in Britain in the 1850s, Europeans started to postulate African inferiority and to treat Africans and their practices as "barbaric." These, they said, came from primitive mentality, and should, therefore, be replaced with elements of Western civilization.[15] Christians, naturally, rejected the evolutionary concept, of Darwinism; but they accepted the aspects that dealt with African inferiority and the need to replace some of their culture. African converts appeared even more destructive of the African belief system and institutions than the whites. With vigour, they went out to condemn and smash such institutions. The House of Skulls was not spared. Whether it was in Brass, in Andoni, Bonny, Kalabari, Nembe, Okrika or Arochukwu, the fate of these cults was the same.

The case of Brass needs a special mention as it illustrated the multi-faceted nature of the institution. Nembe-Brass people controlled the entire central Niger Delta in terms of the overseas trade, selling slaves, palm oil, etc., to the European traders at Akassa, Brass, etc. But once European traders had discovered that the Niger River emptied its waters into the Atlantic ocean, such traders started to move into the interior. In the process, they seized markets that had traditionally belonged to Brass men.

Naturally, the Brass men complained and when they were tired of complaining, they invaded the Royal Niger Company factories at Akassa, killing and taking captives of many company officials[15] who could not escape. This was the subject matter of E.J. Alagoa's *The Small Brave City-State* (Madison, University of Wisconsin Press, 1964).

The significance of this victory for *Egbesu* was obvious. Before long, *Egbesu*, the Brass House of Skulls, was enlarged with new skulls from the raid.[16] This was enough excuse for the destruction of the structure. By 1906, it was no longer in existence.

In a similar move, the Andoni House of Skulls was destroyed. Mr. A. A. Whitehouse, a Vice-Consul for the Bight of Benin and Biafra landed in Andoni in 1904 in a "Gun-boat" at the head of a "small escort" of officers and burnt down the House of Skulls with its over 2,000 skulls.[19] When Whitehouse came for the job initially, there were signs of movement of Obolo (Andoni) people to counter the destruction of the House of Skulls. Whitehouse had to withdraw and return three days later with the reinforcement described above, as well as an addition of Bonny and Opobo war-canoes.

Whitehouse tried several times to set fire to the house but the house failed to ignite. He then removed his helmet and called on God, apparently, for divine intervention and thereafter the House ignited and that was the end of the Andoni House of Skulls. He also carried away valuable artifacts from the shrine of *Yok-Obolo,* including a bronze image of a man which the people claimed was the image of Obolo himself and another, a large bell with the inscription. "Otto Bakker Rotadammo 1757" which showed that the people traded with Rotterdam; and others.

And finally, the Kalabari House of Skulls. In Kalabari, King Amakiri IV was an extremely tradition-oriented monarch and despite the effort and dedication of Rev, W. Carew, Assistant to Bishop Crowther, the King followed the dictation of the So *Alabo* (High Priest) of *Okpolodo.* Also, Kalabari children whom the King allowed to embrace the

Christian religion were, in fact, not for Christianity but for the secret of the palm oil trade. Tired of their failure to convert Kalabari people to Christianity,, the CMS moved to Okrika in 1885 where they eventually established St. Peters Church. The acceptance of Christianity by the Kalabari people and the destruction of the House of Skulls came much later.

By the Brussels Act of 1890's, the British had placed restrictions on the importation of fire-arms into the Niger Delta. The Brussels Act which came into force in 1894, was, among other things, designed to weaken the military base of the native states and those of them like Andoni, Opobo, Bonny, etc., that already acquired arms, were made to give up such arms and ammunitions. In this way, the British ensured that the fear that the "strong native power" may become stronger and difficult to control, was put to rest.[8]

5.3 The Relevance of the House of Skulls
The focus of this work is the origin, function and collapse of the House of Skulls. The movement

evident in the process of evolution, growth and collapse of the cult is historical. Also historical is our insistence that the cult must be studied against the background of the time and period when it developed. But, the subject matter of culture is one that some may argue is the exclusive preserve of the anthropologist. Even so is the methodology that emphasized the use of oral tradition, the collection of which is a matter for the present.

Inter-disciplinary approach to history allows us to do so for, by it, we are able to appreciate better the inter-dependence of history and anthropology in the study of culture and history. By it, also, the past and the present can be seen as continuous, one, helping toward a better understanding of the other. All these have implications for the study of a dead culture like the House of Skulls.

The House of Skulls has come and gone. Like human sacrifice, twin-killing, and other customs practised by Africans, the House of Skulls was brushed aside for more civilized methods of solving the problems of the Niger Delta environment. The fact that some regarded it as revolting raises the question of why one should even bother to study the institution. From the discussion so far, it is easy to say that such study enables us to appreciate the present for it is essential for an understanding of the past. It is impossible to appreciate the present culture unless we are also able to appreciate the stages of development of a particular culture. We would think that this is the factor that explains the continuous study of Medieval witchcraft, alchemy and other practices that are either dead or being replaced by pure science. Europeans groped for solutions to the problem of their environment until such efforts stimulated the ideas that informed the 17th/18th century enlightenment. Even now, the story of the killing and suffering in Kosovo is a reality. Instruments of mass destruction of life are being unleashed in rapid alternation and, with it, the perfection in the skill and in the designs for destruction of human life.

Although the Andoni House of Skulls emerged

from the people's concern for their dead heroes, it soon changed meaning when European traders came and described it as an image of power of the Andoni. Even the Andoni themselves started seeing it as such, and allowed the new meaning to stand because it was more profitable to taste power at that time when power came from victory in war; and victory in war ensured the monopoly of the political and economic advantages of the environment. Is it surprising that those Delta city-states that had the houses of skulls were also the most powerful and feared? The British spent so much time and energy, preparing the invasion of the shrine of *Ibiniukpabi* (Long Juju) because of the image of power symbolized by the size of the Aro House of Skulls. So, if we are to understand the present, we have to understand the past, the past and present being two sides of a coin.

Also, warfare, symbolized by the House of Skulls, is still with us. Some communities in the Niger Delta are still irridentist in their inter-communal relations, making the factors of war and peace constant factors in such inter-communal relations. From the above observations, the House of Skulls informs us that the problems of power, dominance and wealth are still with the Niger Delta people, and Igbo hinterland.

Notes

1. The example of Bishop Samuel Ajayi Crowther is worthy of note. He served selflessly in the Niger Delta and was respected by both Africans and Europeans. With the advent of the new imperialism, he was jettisoned because he was an African. E. A. Ayandele, *The Missionary Impact on Modern Nigeria* (London, Longman, 1966).
2. Barbot (Paris, 1732), pp. 462-463.
3. Elspeth Huxley, *Four Guineas* (London, Reprint Society, 1954), p. 283quoted in Epelle, *op. cit.*, p.2. For details, see Alan Burns *History of Nigeria* (London, 1978), p. 147, 2.

4. K.O. Dike, *Trade and Politics in the Niger Delta* (Oxford, 1956).
5. Dike, *op. cit.* Also, A.E. Afigbo, *African Civilization* (London, 1971), pp. 143-144; Dike, *op. cit.*, p.46 where, in terms of "cunning" in trade, the Kalabari were compared with the Jews or Chinese. See also P.A. Talbot, *People of Southern Nigeria* Vol. 1 (1926),
6. Ejituwu, *op. cit.* (Port Harcourt 1991).
7. Baikie, *op cit.*, p. 313, *British Pioneers in West Africa* (London, nd).
8. *Ibid.*
9. J.C. Anene, *Southern Nigeria in Transition* (London, 1966).
10. Hope Waddell, *op. cit.* Africans may be barbaric, but Europeans were not less so. Their common involvement in the trans-Atlantic slave trade is still fresh in mind. The abolition of the slave trade in the early decades of the 19th C gave them moral superiority and by 1900, Victorian England had started to perceive themselves as culturally elevated to the level of the angels. But

(the First World War, and even more of the Second World War, showed that man, whether Black or White, was essentially animalistic). Europeans who inflicted at Verdun (1916) on themselves, with Britain alone losing over 20,000 men a day and over 1 million people dead in the battle, cannot claim to be superior to the African. The said civilization was only skin-deep. See John Steele Gordon, "What We Lost in the Great War," *American Heritage*, July/August *(1992)*. Also, see Alan Bullock *Hitler: A Study in Tyranny* (Reading, 1981).

11. Alagoa, *op. cit.* (1972), p. 154, fn. 2.
12. Comte C.N. de Cardi, "A Short Description of the Natives of the Niger Coast Protectorate," *West African Studies* (London, 1899), pp. 443-556.
13. British Parliamentary Paper, Vol. 74 (1888 c. 53651).
14. Philip Curtin, *Daedalus* (Spring, 1974), pp. 17-29.
15. G.N. Uzoigwe, "European Partition and Conquest of Africa: An Overview," *General History of Africa*, Vol. VII (London, 1984), pp. 19-

44). Brian Tierney, Donald Kagan and L. Peasrse Williams, *Great Issues in Western Civilization*, Vol. II, (New York, 1976), pp. 327-370. These changes are inevitable and are taking place before our own eyes. In the pre-colonial times, an average youth in the study area must go to war and earn glory through his martial skill (like the North American Indian youth who must scalp a whiteman) to be regarded as having come of age. Then education came with Christianity and an average Nigerian youth was expected to earn the West African School Certificate (WASC) to be regarded as progressive and as having a future. Today, it is university education. But, even then, one is no longer too sure as the latter, in many cases, cannot fetch commensurate remunerations and, in some communities, a shift from education to business and money-making is taking place. This, indeed, is the subject of history, the study of change and continuity. For head-hunting by American Indian youth, see S.E. Morrison *Oxford History of the American*

People (Oxford, 1965). And for a similar situation among the Igbo, see Elizabeth Isichei, *Igbo Worlds* (London, 1977).

16. A. Burns, *History of Nigeria* (London, 1978), p.165.

17. *Ibid.* A.E. Afigbo, "The Eclipse of the Aro Slaving Oligarchy, 1901-1927" *Journal of the Historical Society of Nigeria,* Vol. 6, No. 1, December 1971, pp. 3-24.

18. J.U.J. Asiegbu, *Nigeria and its British Invaders* (New York, 1984), pp. 237-238. Also, Ajayi, J. Ade and M. Crowder (1974), p. 408.

19. A.A. Whitehouse "An African Fetish," *Journal of African Studies* (London, 1904), pp. 410-416. Also, Cypril Aldred, "A, Bronze Cult Object from Southern Nigeria," *Man,* No. 47 (1949), pp. 38-39. Andoni was divided into six parts and each part was placed in one of the six different court areas to ensure that Andoni cultural unity was destroyed. M.D.W. Jeffreys described this as "the ghastly policy pursued in the administration of Andoni" "Intelligence

Report on Andoni (1930)". He came to Nigeria as a young man in 1915 and died in about 1975. See Paul Gabaur, "In Memoriam: Dr. M.D.W. Jeffreys" in *The Nigerian Fields*, Vol. XL, 4 (1975), pp. 191-192.

20. J.F. Ade Ajayi and Michael Crowder, *West African History*. Vol. II (London, 1974), p. 408.

21. John Steele Gordon, "What We Lost in the Great War." *American Heritage*, July/August, 1992.

CHAPTER 6

Conclusion

6.1 Summary

This is a study of the House of Skulls, one of the lost cultures of the Niger Delta. Started probably in Obolo (Andoni),, it (the House of Skulls) spread to other parts of the Niger Delta and Igbo hinterland.[1] In Andoni where it started, it was meant as a memoriam of Andoni men killed in the war with the Ohafia. But the meaning changed when European visitors to Andoni began to describe it as a House containing the skulls of Andoni enemies killed in war[2]; and, because it immediately conjured an image of power and economic fortune, it was allowed to stand. This meaning became very popular and attractive and, before long, other people, competing with the Obolo (Andoni) in the same environment, soon started indiscriminate acquisition of "heads" and subsequently their erection of huge Houses of Skulls.

Bonny and Kalabari built the biggest ones, following the importance and awe attached to it by the European traders whom the Delta middlemen depended on for economic survival and power.[3] It is doubtful that Bonny and Kalabari knew that Obolo (Andoni) original intention was to immortalize and memorialize their fallen heroes in a battle with the Ohafia. Europeans came and bastardized the practice and the concept of the House of Skulls [4] It is possible that even the Obolo (Andoni) began to assume that the House of Skulls was the symbol of warfare when Europeans generally accepted it as such.

In the hinterland, the concept became even more profitable. The Aro built around themselves an image of power. In those days the Shrine *of Ibiniukpabi* was visited even by Delta people once there was problem of identification. For instance, a man or woman accused of witchcraft must go to Arochukwu to clear him/herself and the Aro took advantage of the situation and built a formidable House of Skulls by "cunning" and "deceit."[5] Soon

Arochukwu became a household name in the entire Eastern Niger Delta.

6.2 Conclusion

The House of Skulls has come and gone. But the questions raised by its existence are still with us. One may ask whether war has ended or whether man's inhumanity to man has stopped? Of course, violence and brutality are still with us, making the House of Skulls still relevant. We have merely isolated the modern era, the era of petroleum and petro-dollar, from the work, to enable us focus on the issue of the House of Skulls, with its implications for moral decadence. This, indeed, is the meaning of the violence represented by the activities of the "Militants" in the Niger Delta which, for methodological convenience, we have decided not to accommodate in this work.[6]

Social psychologist, William McDougal (1871-1938), traced war to an instinct of pugnacity and William James (1842-1910) hoped that peaceful competition like football and sports generally would gradually replace conflict and that the state would find a "moral equivalent" of war by drafting young men for socially useful projects. Violent emotion can be sublimated by sports or by reading books, watching movies, or television programmes, dealing with war and violence.

Psychologists like Ivan Parlov (1849-1939) studied state education for violence on the basis that societies have always regarded some forms of violence as good, such, for instance, as trained soldiers and mobile police. These pioneer psychologists were merely applying scientific analysis to well known social phenomena. The modern soldier may be more likely to develop combat neuroses or psychoses than the soldier of the past and some of these can be treated.

These issues are not new and the United Nations has been considering them since the end of the Second World War, hoping that it would provide answers to them, not only for the Niger Delta and its hinterland but for the world as a whole.[7]

However, one would have wished that colonialism had allowed African practices to stand and mature to see whether, like the European example, they would have given rise to such enlightenment which blossomed into the Industrial Revolution of the 19th century. This wish is not new. In his book, *Colonialism and Alienation* (trans. William Feuser and published by Benin City: Ethiope Publishing Company, 1969), Franz Fanon raised the issue. An African, in a colonial situation, is like a man with a "Black skin and a White mask;" he is a savage, not in a cannibalistic sense but in the sense of lacking in refinement [8].

That is not all. Ms Rosamond Burgi, a French Lecturer at Yankton College, Yankton, South Dakota, USA, used to tell this writer that many in the USA wished that colonialism had left the African culture alone, for by interfering with thee African cultures, colonialism cut the African from his cultural root; and, since he had not the European environment to learn the colonial super-imposition (European culture), he was left dangling: he was schizophrenic.[9]

And finally, again, the above wish is not new. The All African Festival of Arts and Cultures (Festac '77), held in Lagos, wished that colonialism had left the African cultures alone. However, by the Festac, the African should be aware that he had arts and cultures which were destroyed by colonialism. He should not forget them.

Notes

1. Barbot, *op. cit.* (Paris, 1732), pp 462-463.

2. K.O. Dike, *Trade and Politics in the Niger Delta* (Oxford, 1956). Also, G.I.Jones, *The Trading States of the Oil Rivers* (Cambridge, 1963).

3. Nkparom C. Ejituwu, *A History of Obolo (Andoni) in the Niger Delta* (Oron and University of Port Harcourt Press, 1991). Also, Paul U.Ndukwe, *op, cit.* (Port Harcourt, 1985).

4. Baikie, *op cit.* (London, 1856), pp. 313-316, 413.

5. The Andoni regarded the Ohafia as their

"brothers." During important occasions, the Andoni would invite them. Such occasions as *Nkwak* (victory war-dance) would inevitably bring the Ohafia to Andoni.Oral sources say that some Ohafia people are trying to locate their roots in Andoni. Also, see Paul U. Ndukwe of Ohafia (c. 50) in a personal communication published in Nkparom C. Ejituwu, *A History of the Obolo (Andoni) in the Niger Delta* (Oron and University of Port Harcourt, (1991), pp. 256-257.

6. Nnah B. Barinem, "Towards a Holistic Peace Process for the Niger Delta" (MA. Thesis, University of Port Harcourt, (2008).
7. Brian Tierney, *et al.*, *Great Issues in Western Civilization*, Vol. II (New York.1976), pp. 307-343.
8. Renate Zahar, *Colonialism and Alienation* (trans. W. Feuser) (Ethiope) Publishing Company, 1969), p. 52.
9. Ms. Rosamond Burgi of Yankton College, South Dakota, USA, in a personal communication, 1969.

References

A. Primary Sources

Adaka, Augustus (Chief) (c. 70) Clan Head of Eastern Obolo, interviewed on December, 1974.

Abam, A.S. (Chief/Dr.) in a personal communication, Port Harcourt, 2 October, 1992.

Akwa, Stephen (Chief) (c. 75), Traditional Head of Okoroete, interviewed on December 31, 1974.

Brown, Brown (Chief) of Unyeada at Otu-Afu (Andoni), 1974.

Ekenekot, U.O. (Chief) (c. 65) of Ama Adaka, interviewed on December 26, 1975.

Ekoh, Matthew (Chief) (c. 80), High Priest of *Yok-Obolo*, interviewed at Agwut Obolo, April 28, 1974.

Ekpoke. Titus Okurube (Chief) (c. 80) of Okoroete, interviewed on December 30, 1974.

Feuser, William (Professor) of the University of Port Harcourt in a personal communication, June 13, 1992. Professor Feuser was a German and a veteran of the Second World War; he had first hand information on the brutality of the War which was incomparable to anything Africans have done.

Ikuru, Dixon A.E. (Chief) (c. 60) of Ikuru Town, Andoni, interviewed in 1980.

Iraron, Lot (Chief) of Egwede (c. 70), Chairman, Andoni Council of Chiefs, Ngo, Andoni, 1989.

Ndukwe, Paul U. of Ohafia (c.50) in a personal communication, Port Harcourt, 27 August, 1985.

Nsirem, Benjamin (Chief) of Agana (c.80), Andoni (1975).

Odiari., Simeon of Ikuru Town (c. 106) was informative on Obolo and their neighbours (1950).

Otoko, Dixon C. (Chief) of Alabie, Andoni, December 1974,

Ogbolikan, Job (Chief) of Dema Andoni, 1974.

Opu-Ogulaya, E.D.W. (Chief) in a personal communication, Port Harcourt, 1975.

Ukafia, Owen (Chief) of Okoroete, Chairman, Akwa Ibom State Council of Chiefs, Uyo, 1996.

B. Secondary Sources

Abasiattai, Monday, *A History of the Cross River Region of Nigeria* (Enugu, 1990) where Isaac Parker (European trader in Calabar accompanied an Erik Chief in 1765 on a slave-catching expedition in the Cross River area).

Afigbo, A.E., "The Eclipse of the Aro Oligarchy" in *The Igbo and Their Neighbours* (Ibadan, 1987).

Alagoa, E.J., *A History of the Niger Delta* (Ibadan, 1972).

Alagoa, E.J., *The Small Brave City State* (Madison, 1964).

Alagoa, E.J. and A. Fombo, *A Chronicle of Grand Bonny* (Ibadan, 1972).

Aldred, Cyril, "A Bronze Cult Object from Southern Nigeria," *MAN*, No. 47 (1949), pp. 38-39.

Amadi, Elechi, *Ethics in Nigerian Culture* (London, Heinemann, 1984).

Anderson, Martha, "From Adumu to Mami Wata: Central Jjo Water Spirit Imagery" in *The Multi-Disciplinary Approach to African History* (ed.) Nkparom C. Ejituwu (University of Lagos Press,

1997), pp. 257-275.

Anderson, Martha, "Central Ijo Shrines and Spirits" A paper presented at the Faculty of Humanities Seminar Series, January 30, 1992.

Anene, J.C. *Southern Nigeria in Transition* (London, 1966).

Arua, A.O., *A Short History of Ohafla* (Enugu, Omnibus, 1951).

Baikie, William, *Narrative of an Exploring Voyage* (London, 1956).

British Parliamentary Paper, Vol. 74 (1988 C. 53651).

Burns, Alan, *A History of Nigeria* (London, 1978).

Cookey, S.J.S., *King Jaja of the Niger Delta* (New York, 1974).

Croce as quoted in R.H. Carr, *What is History?* (London, 1984).

Curtin, P.D., *The Image of Africa* (Madison, 1964).

Curtin, P.D., *Daedalus* (Spring, 1974), pp. 17-29.

Dapper, Olfert, *Description of Africa* (Amsterdam, 1778).

De Cardi, Comte C.N. "A Short Description of the

Natives of the Coast Protectorate" in Mary Kingsley, *West African Studies* (London, 1899), pp. 443-556.

De Cardi, Comte C.N. "Andoni River and Its Inhabitants" in Mary Kingsley, *West African Studies* (London, 1899), pp. 538-540.

Dike, K.O., *Trade and Politics in the Niger Delta, 1830-1885* (Oxford, 1956).

Dike, K.O. and Felicia Ekejiuba, *The Aro of South-Eastern Nigeria- 1650-1950* (Ibadan, 1990).

Ejituwu, Nkparom C., "Warfare and Diplomacy in the Niger Delta" in Toyin Falola and Robin Law, *Warfare and Diplomacy in Pre-colonial Nigeria* (Wisconsin, 1992), pp. 199-207.

Ejituwu, Nkparom C., "Yok-Obolo: The Influence of a Traditional Religion on the Socio-Cultural Life of the Andoni People" in *AFRICA Journal of the Institute of African Studies*, Vol. 65, 1 (1995), pp. 997-113.

Ejituwu, Nkparom C., "Andoni-Bonny Treaty of 1846: A Diplomatic Curiosity," *ODU: Journal of West African Studies*, Vol. 36 (July 1989), pp.

57-74.

Ejituwu, Nkparom C., "The Political Economy of the Andoni-Bonny Treaty of 1846" in Yakubu A. Ochefa (ed.), *Oral Traditions, Totems and Nigerian Cultural History* (Aboki Publication, 2003), pp. 55-76.

Epelle, E.M. *The Church in the Niger Delta* (Aba, 1972).

Erekosima, Tonye V., *Cultural Institution* (Port Harcourt, 1989) (the unedited version).

Ereforokuma, Peter, "Andoni in Diaspora" (University of Port Harcourt BA Hons History Project, 1992).

Fanon, Franz, *Colonialism and Alienation* (France, 1969).

Gordon, John Steele, "What We Lost in the Great War," *Heritage* (America, July-August, 1992).

Harlett, Robin, *Africa*, Vol. 1 (London, 1970.

Ikuru, Raph O. Manuscript *Brief History of Obolo (Andoni)* (Ikuru Town, 1953).

Isichei, Elizabeth, *Igbo Worlds* (London, 1977).

Jeffreys, M.D.W., "Intelligence Report on the Andoni

(1930)," NA/E CP 7237 Minloc 6/1/135).

Jones, G.I., *The Trading States of the Oil Rivers* (Cambridge, 1963).

Kalu, Jennifer E., "A History of Ohafia" (University of Port Harcourt B.A. Hons Project, 2008).

Leonard, A.G., *The Lower Niger Delta and Its Tribes* (London, 1906).

Ndukwe, Paul U., "Settlement Pattern and Social Structure of the Ohafia" (University of Port Harcourt B.Sc. (Sociology) Project, 1985).

Nsugbe, Philip O., "Oron Ekpo Figures" in *Nigeria Magazine*, Vol. 71 (1961), pp, 357-359.

Nzimiro, Ikenna. *Studies in Ibo Political System* (Berkeley, Los Angeles, 1972).

Onwuzirike, E.A., "Mbaise under Colonial Rule" (University of Port Harcourt PhD Dissertation, 1992).

Opugulaya, E.D.W., *A Cultural Heritage of the Wakirike People* (Port Harcourt, 1975).

Pereira, Pachecco, *Esmeraldo de Situ Orbis* (trans.) G.H.T. Kimble (London, 1937), p.132.

Talbot, P.A. *People of Southern Nigeria,* Vol. I (London, 1926).

Tieracy, Brian, Donald Kegan and L. Pearse, William, *Great Issues in Western Civilization,* Vol. II (New York, 1976), pp. 307-343.

Uka, N. " A Note on Abam Warriors of Igboland" in *Ikenga* Vol. 1,2 (1972), pp. 76-82 in M. Noah and T. Ekpo, *Warfare and Diplomacy in Ibibioland* (1972).

Uya, Okon E., *A History of Oron People* (Uyo, 1984).

Uzoigwe. G.N., *Britain and the Conquest of Africa* (Ann Arbor, 1974).

Waddell, Hope, *Twenty Nine Years in the West Indies and Central Africa* (London, 1963).

Webber, H. "Intelligence Report on Bonny Tribe" (1931) (NA/1 CSO. 26 27226), p.28.

Whitehouse, A.A., "An African Fetish" *Journal of African Studies* (London, 1904), pp. 410-416.

Williamson, Kay, "Languages of the Lower Niger Delta," *Nigeria Magazine,* 97 (1968), 124-130.

Printed in the United States
By Bookmasters